Cognitive Behavioural Therapy

A Simple Step-by-Step Guide to Managing Fear, Anxiety, Depression and Stress by Challenging Unwanted Thoughts

By Adrian Kirk

sell, use, quote or paraphrase any part, or the content within this book, without the consent of the author or publisher.

Disclaimer Notice:

Please note the information contained within this document is for educational and entertainment purposes only. All effort has been executed to present accurate, up to date, and reliable, complete information. No warranties of any kind are declared or implied. Readers acknowledge that the author is not engaging in the rendering of legal, financial, medical or professional advice. The content within this book has been derived from various sources. Please consult a licensed professional before attempting any techniques outlined in this book.

By reading this document, the reader agrees that under no circumstances is the author responsible for any losses, direct or indirect, which are incurred as a result of the use of information contained within this document, including, but not limited to, — errors, omissions, or inaccuracies.

Table of Contents

Introduction

In our modern-day society, it is easy to be swept up in achieving and acquiring the best of everything. The best cars, the biggest houses, and the most amazing holiday destinations.

With the advent of social media, we are exposed to lifestyles that are overtly lavish, brimming with success and happiness, all in the name of increasing the follower count. Just do not show the credit card bills.

We compare ourselves to those people we see on these social pages and are left found wanting because we feel we do not quite measure up. We feel pressured to keep up with what society has labeled as the hottest and most successful trends.

Feelings of inadequacy, social pressures and other issues that impact self-esteem (which could be highlighted through social media) are some of the risk factors related to increased rates of suicides among the youth. Another factor, which is especially prevalent on social media (MFMER, no date), as of late is acceptance and acknowledgment of personal sexual preference and identity.

In recent years the #mentalhealthmatters movement has taken hold and has grown in the online community.

While there is an improvement and acceptance among the community, especially where mental health is prioritized (or attempted at the very least), the risks of developing mental health issues such as stress, anxiety, and depression is still present.

There are numerous books that attempt to teach

us about the need to disconnect from the things in life that cause us distress and for good reason. With the increased interest in mental health, people are becoming more and more aware of the external factors that have always had an impact on our personal, mental and physical well-being but was muted by the ruling thought in society that the "no pain, no gain" mindset is the mindset of the strong.

In a society where strength is idolized, any form of weakness is shunned or locked away. This certainly includes mental health disturbances, which in the long run had catastrophic effects on the mental wellbeing of society as a whole.

Suddenly, as you peruse through endless Tweets, it would appear as though there are a lot more people with mental disorders "cropping up". It isn't solely due to the fact that there certainly may be an increase in the occurrence of these people but more accurately, that only now are people starting to feel that it is okay to come forward with their problems and seek help openly, unashamedly.

However, even with the rise in acceptance among their peers, the pressure of being "normal" is still a present threat.

With the help of therapy, one's internal stresses could be minimized or in some cases be removed completely.

Where some are unable to afford the visit to a psychologist whether it is due to financial constraints or location limitations, cognitive behavioral therapy exists at a level that is accessible to many.

This book is a guide to help bridge the gap that exists between mental health care and affordability in a meaningful and effective way.

Cognitive behavioral therapy is meant to educate each individual on how to identify and manage emotions, thoughts and the resulting actions, provided that the exercises are practiced frequently, and logging progress is taken seriously. This program should take approximately eight weeks to complete although this is just a guideline.

However, you do not need to feel pressured to keep with the schedule. The idea is that you follow at your own pace in order to get the most out of this book. The effectiveness of this program is predicated on willingness and dedication; additionally, you can complete it along with a friend or family member and that is okay.

In this book, I will be covering a couple of mental and emotional issues such as stress and depression. I will explain what cognitive behavioral therapy is, why it is useful and how it can help you to become familiar with the topic.

I also provide a breakdown of several causes of negative thoughts and emotions and how to deal with them.

Additionally, you will find a selection of exercises, tips, tricks and ideas on how to get the most out of his guide; as well as strategies that you could utilize in order to manage your negative emotions and thoughts.

Chapter 1: Cognitive Behavioral Therapy?

"Transforming one's thoughts will ultimately result in positive action and behavior in difficult moments."

~Greta Gleisner

What is Cognitive Behavioral Therapy?

"Have you ever kept a gratitude journal? What about monitoring your donut intake? Have you tracked your daily steps or monitored your sleep? Then you are already applying some of the principles of CBT in your everyday life." (Howes, 2017)

What is Psychotherapy?

To understand cognitive behavioral therapy let us first take a look at psychotherapy.

Psychotherapy, otherwise known as talk therapy, is only one of many ways that assists people who suffer from a wide variety of both mental health and emotional difficulties in identifying, addressing, and controlling symptoms linked with these illnesses.

During sessions of psychotherapy, several approaches are looked into in order to optimize treatment on an individual basis. More often than not, psychotherapy can help increases a person's understanding and management of their mental and emotional distress.

For non-severe or serious mental health difficulties, psychotherapy is the first choice for treatment given that it could potentially produce results from the first session.

What is Cognitive Behavioral Therapy?

Unlike certain other psychotherapy treatments, cognitive behavioral therapy mainly deals with a person's current problems, rather than focusing on those from your past.

Cognitive behavioral therapy, or CBT, is a psychotherapy technique focused on identifying and reprogramming, or changing, negative thoughts that lead to self-destructive behaviors in a chosen time frame.

It is a technique that can help you manage your problems simply by changing the way you think and behave.

Cognitive behavioral therapy places emphasis on our *thinking* as one of the biggest factors that affect how you end up responding to certain events in your life, in terms of your emotional and behavioral responses. (Beck, 1976). Meaning that your thoughts affect emotions, emotions affect behavior and behavior can "reward" thoughts and cause them to solidify or become permanent, making it difficult to change them.

CBT nurtures the idea that the way we think about or understand how we experience life events, has a massive effect on how we end up *feeling* about said experiences and events. Logically then, thoughts and beliefs strongly influence behavioral patterns.

It also suggests that these thoughts and their matching emotional responses have a tendency to become routine or second nature over the course of one's life.

Another major point in cognitive behavioral therapy is that because we are aware of our thoughts in a specific moment, we are able to choose a different action in order to change the outcome. By being increasingly aware of and recognizing emotions and reactions we are able to lead more functional and healthier lives.

The ultimate goal of cognitive behavioral therapy is to address and replace negative thoughts and behaviors or actions with thoughts and behaviors that will make the individual feel well equipped to tackle any difficult situation that may arise.

CBT helps people identify and change "bad" or negative thought patterns and actions and then replacing these patterns with ones that are more grounded and useful in self-healing. It forces you to focus on one aspect of your problem at a time and how to resolve them or at the very least reduce the negative effect these problems have on your day-to-day life.

Given that the issues addressed are generally not overly severe, this form of treatment is the first choice for many, as it is time and cost effective.

How does CBT work

Cognitive behavioral therapy is most commonly used to treat anxiety, depression, and severe stress, but can be useful for other mental and physical health problems which also range from eating disorders to phobias.

CBT looks at negative thoughts that lead to a

negative cycle, where these thoughts lead to feelings that lead to negative actions that lead to negative thoughts. See where I'm going with this?

By changing one aspect of the cycle, you divert this cycle and create change. This means that mental issues such as anxiety and depression are broken down into more manageable chunks. In this way, CBT allows you to take control and introduce more positive thoughts and actions into your life.

Cognitive behavioral therapy provides you with the tools in which to identify and challenge unhelpful and unrealistic thoughts. It provides you with the problem-solving skills required to address and remedy these thoughts to create a better outcome.

It teaches identification of trouble areas alongside

problem solving and behavioral adaptation through exposure; CBT re-trains certain social skills and teaches relaxation techniques.

In order for cognitive behavioral therapy to be effective, it requires practice - while other psychotherapies often require the same, note that CBT takes less time overall than its counterparts. Even though the time required to recognize results is greatly reduced (as compared to other therapy types (Anderson, 2019)) it still requires a form of commitment from the user.

Let us take a brief look at the following as an example:

You have made plans with a friend. They have canceled a few times, but you keep trying. Even as a person that has no mental/social hiccup in this department, something like this does have a tendency to stick in one's craw. However, *how* you accept and deal with the information is what matters.

A normal brain will respond in a way similar to this:

I accept that they have canceled on me (yet again, or maybe a first offense, but I was really looking forward to having a good day out with them regardless). Yes, I have the right to be upset. I acknowledge this. I may stay angry for a short while, and perhaps I may even feel a little neglected. However, I will not allow these thoughts to fester. I *decide* that it isn't a particularly big deal. We reschedule and I make plans with another friend or even go out alone.

I did not let the situation get the best of me and I acknowledged that they did not cancel because of spite or out of malice.

Here is the same situation, with the same scenario but from the viewpoint of a troubled brain:

You have made plans with a friend. They have canceled a few times, but you keep trying. How do you react when a friend says they cannot go out with you because they are busy? A negative thought linked to this situation could be seen as "they find my company boring" or "they do not really like me".

By believing what your thoughts are telling you about this situation, you create the opportunity for the cycle of negativity to continue. Suddenly, it turns to "maybe nobody actually likes me" or "they must only spend time with me out of pity", which will eventually lead to more thoughts of inadequacy, self-hate, anxiety, and depression;

the result is another night at home, replaying the cycle in your head.

Sometimes to the point where future invitations are rejected because you "do not feel like it" and "why bother, nobody wants me there anyway". When, really, it is just you stuck in a negative loop.

Here's where the magic comes in.

Having now avoided the social setting due to these negative thoughts, the idea of entering a situation that will force you to face the thoughts will create fear. It is normal to want to avoid the things you fear because this reduces your anxiety in the short term.

Cognitive behavioral therapy would have you *identify* the negative thoughts for what they are and address them, encouraging you to dismiss the thoughts by replacing them with more neutral or positive thoughts; listing the ways your friend could truly be busy, followed by a list of people who do like you. In order for this step to be more effective, you will combine it with a similarly positive *action*.

By exposing yourself to these situations in small doses, it will eventually decrease the fear you have of them and with it the negative thoughts associated with them.

The idea behind cognitive behavioral therapy is to *question* all negative assumptions.

You are shown how to change these negative patterns to improve the way you feel.

It looks at ways you can improve your state of mind each day for long-term results.

How to use CBT

Exposure (the term used in cognitive behavioral therapy to name the process by which you challenge your internal negative cycle to effect eventual positive outcomes) involves *gradually* and *repeatedly* entering feared situations until you feel less anxious.

You start with situations that only cause you a little bit of anxiety. In the previous example, you avoided all social gatherings for fear of rejection combined with self-induced self-hate. An example of challenging this *fear* is to go out.

Go grab a cup of coffee, chat with the barista. Next week have drinks after work with a colleague. Take small steps and work your way up to facing things that cause you a greater deal of anxiety.

By changing just one thing, you set the stage for creating a happier lifestyle.

What happens during these CBT sessions?

Usually, you will have a session with your therapist once a week or once every 2 weeks which will last anywhere from 30 minutes to an hour. The duration of your treatment largely depends on the severity of your condition, starting at five sessions going on to 25 sessions.

Using cognitive behavioral therapy from home will definitely require commitment from your part. Set up a schedule. Take *at least* 30 minutes per session. The frequency depends on you.

During these sessions, you will need to break down the problems you have into their separate identifying parts:

(Using the previous example again)

1. Thoughts:

They canceled

I am boring

They do not like me

Nobody likes me.

2. Feelings:

Sadness

Anger

Self-hate

Depression

3. Actions:

You stop going out altogether and compound the situation by extracting yourself from any social event and spiraling deeper into your negative thoughts.

By writing these things down, you have a concrete starting point. You will analyze each category to identify which thoughts/feeling/actions are unreasonable or unrealistic and unhelpful. You will also work out how they interlink with each other and in what ways they affect you.

By using this guide, you will be able to empower yourself to change your own thoughts and behaviors that are causing distress in your life.

Once you have identified the problems and worked out *how* to change them you will be required to *act;* and as we all know, practice makes perfect.

What you aim to learn from this practice is how to apply these skills in your day to day life in order to improve upon it.

This should help you manage your problems and reduce the likeliness that they will have a continuous negative impact on your life, even after your course of treatment finishes.

Chapter 2: Benefits of Cognitive Behavioral Therapy

Some of the advantages of CBT:

1. Identifying negative thoughts
2. Identifying harmful behavior
3. Managing emotions
4. Managing stress
5. Self-healing
6. Coping with grief
7. Remedying sleep problems such as Insomnia
8. Managing pain
9. Managing Fear

10. Alleviating depression and anxiety

11. Controlling eating disorders

12. In certain cases, combining with other therapies in order to increase their effectiveness in dealing with PTSD and addiction

13. Restructuring time management

14. Resolving interpersonal issues

How long does it take to complete a CBT session?

"One of the highlights of CBT is that it is focused on eliminating symptoms as quickly as possible, typically in a few weeks to a few months. Of course, people rarely have only a single issue to work on in therapy, so this length depends on the number and severity of the issues, but brevity is key to this approach."

~ Ryan Howes

Is CBT right for me?

So, you want to try cognitive behavioral therapy? Before deciding to have CBT, it would be helpful to ask yourself the following:[1]

> 1. Am I comfortable thinking about my feelings? Am I comfortable diving right into my own innermost thoughts and feeling and poking around in there? It might get uncomfortable. It might really

---

[1] Mind.org.uk

stir up your anxieties and fears. Be prepared.

2. How much time do I have? How much time am I willing to give for therapy? Because this guide relies on your full participation and commitment to see it through to the end, you may need to set a schedule to ensure the "homework" set out for you is completed.

3. Is short-term psychotherapy like CBT right for me? An important question to ask yourself when contemplating the start of cognitive therapy, is how severe are my problems? Sometimes a short-term structured therapy such as CBT may not be ideal, as you require more time.

4. Cognitive behavioral therapy requires clear

direction. You may find it difficult to see results or even know where to start if you have no particular problem or issue you wish to address. If you have a general feeling of unhappiness, perhaps finding the source would be ideal before beginning a course of CBT.

Chapter 3: Finding the Root Cause

The effectiveness of cognitive behavioral therapy is predicated on being able to identify the sources of stress in your life that are causing your mental upset.

The simplified process of one person reacting to a situation whether real or imagined goes as follows: I think, I feel, I react.

Thoughts, emotions, and actions are an integral part of cognitive behavioral therapy and that is at the core of what CBT aims to address and change - the broken Think/Feel/React response.

What are thoughts?

Thoughts are our mental processes during which we acquire information through various media that define our belief systems. Thoughts from our ideals, ideas, and opinions we hold about certain topics. It affects our experiences and how we see the world.

Thoughts can be cultivated into a permanent attitude, which is the result of practicing or reinforcing certain thoughts over a period of time whether by conscious action or an automatic process.

Although our thoughts are shaped by genetics, parenting styles, the type of experiences you encounter, and the level of education you have; your thoughts are ultimately under your control.

Therefore, you can change them.

What are emotions?

Emotions are the internal responses to events and stimuli, for example, happiness, anger, fear, sadness, or excitement.

Emotions are triggered by external and internal factors that include, but are not limited to, watching a show, reading a book, listening to a song, or by memories and thoughts.

It is widely understood that emotions are largely universal, meaning we all experience them on one degree or another, each individual's experience and understanding of them is different.

Your emotions, thoughts, and sensations are the internal things we doubt sometimes. However, there are things you can ask yourself to get grounded in the moment and to appreciate what it is you are feeling and explore the consequences of these feelings when compared to how others may be seeing the same situation.

Ask:

1. Do I really feel this way or is this an emotion that is expected of me in this situation? Do not judge yourself if it is the latter. Our emotional responses are oftentimes regulated and molded by external factors such as instilled values/culture.

2. Should I feel this way and is it the *right* thing to feel, even if it inconveniences other people? You feel sad because you have failed your driver's test. People around you are okay for the first few hours, thereafter they appear increasingly annoyed because, "why are you still upset, get over it." To you, it is a big deal. It would have meant a certain degree of freedom; you studied hard. All that stress during the whole process

seems redundant.

Remember that your emotions are valid, even if other people are inconvenienced by them. It is the actions that you follow up these emotions with that need to be regulated.

Emotions are the strings that bind us on a social level. They can help us create and maintain lasting, healthy relationships if we learn how to use and interpret them.

Emotion regulation:

Why do I need to learn how to regulate my emotions? It is essential to quiet the body. High emotion leads to high stress and anxiety, by quieting your mind and your body, you are able to find the wise mind - the part of you that balances what you know and what you feel.

You will be more equipped in meeting your goals. You will be able to improve your self-respect as you know where your boundaries and limitations lie.

Healthy perspectives on emotions are essential because we cannot remove emotions from the world. They are neither good nor bad. They cannot be compared to another person's version of the same emotion.

Having an emotion (specifically a negative one) is not the same as acting on that emotion. It is okay to have emotions, it is what you do with the information that determines the outcome of the situation or event. However, emotions are not facts. If you feel that you are unwanted or unappreciated, that is just a feeling, it does not necessarily make it true.

Emotions do not last forever; they change and act like the currents on a river. They will come and go, strong and weak. Whenever a particularly strong emotion comes to the surface, it does not mean that you are required to act on it.

Not responding to a negative situation could turn out to be the best for your emotional state and in the long run, your mental health.

There are eight primary emotions: namely; anger, sorrow, joy, fear, disgust, guilt/shame, interest, and surprise.

These emotions are built into our hard-wiring. All humans feel these eight emotions in varying degrees and in different combinations. These combinations are what we refer to as secondary emotions.

They are reaction emotions. Reactive based on input by one of the primary eight. For example, you may feel shame when you experience fear.

The most important thing to note is that these secondary emotions are NOT instinctive. They are taught, they are learned.

There are often additional emotions that go hand in hand with the secondary one depending on how you were raised, in terms of your family values and cultural beliefs.

You could be afraid of spiders. You see one and react negatively by killing it or being aggressive towards others nearby.

The aggression response is tied to fear. After acting out aggressively you may feel shame that you had killed the spider or treated your friends or others with disrespect.

The shame is tied to the action of disrespect, which is tied to the emotion of anger, which is tied to the primary emotion of fear.

Sometimes these secondary emotions can be a bit confusing to work through, but by practicing the skills of differentiating between the two types, you will become better at spotting them and be able to adapt your reactions and emotions.

When you experience a secondary emotion, sit down and figure out which primary feeling triggered the secondary one.

Use your journal to write down your process. Start with the secondary and back-track. Often you will notice the behavioral response before you realize the emotions that are attached. As the example illustrates above, it may be incredibly overwhelming at first; however, all emotions are important and help us in the end.

Emotions basically have three jobs:

1. Communicate.

Emotions are communicated primarily through facial expressions and these nonverbal cues are quick and often uncontrollable.

2. Motivation.

Through emotions, we are able to stay focused and be motivated in any given situation. They instruct us on how to act. Without emotions, we may not be able to react in the correct manner when faced with danger, I.e. running away from a tiger in fear.

3. Automatic.

Emotions are often automatic - we do not have to think about the situation, especially one in which our lives may be at risk. Strong emotions help us overcome obstacles we have set ourselves in our mind, as well as obstacles we may face in our environment.

Unique responses:

Since each of our reactions to certain emotions may be different, we often also experience the emotions to varying degrees of intensity. When working through your own emotions, remember that it is not helpful to compare yourself to others' progress - even if they are experiencing the same kind of emotions and the same kind of situations.

Have courage and know that your pace is set by your own success and ability to adapt. It does not mean you are not making progress.

Letting go of emotional suffering. Practice removing yourself from the emotion. First, observe the emotion. Take a step back and do not feel as though you are part of it but fully experience it for what it is. If it is anger, feel the burn in your stomach or chest (we each regard an emotion in a different way - which means that I could feel anger in my chest, and you could feel it coil in your stomach).

It will come and go like a wave, do not block the emotion or reject it. Do not hold on to the emotion and let it linger.

Remember: You are not your emotion, you do not need to defend it. Do not act on the emotion.

It will take some time, but practice respecting the emotion. It a primal part of who you are and how you manage it, is what will define you. Respect the power that it has.

Changing emotions are complex. They may not be easily identifiable, and they may present as more than one at a time. However, we can change them by simplifying their effect and accompanying behavior. Keep in mind that THERE IS ALWAYS MORE THAN ONE TRUE WAY TO SEE A SITUATION. 6 PLUS THREE IS 9 BUT 3 TIMES 3 IS ALSO 9.

How to cope with and change certain emotions:

1. FEAR. Do what you are afraid of over and over until you become desensitized to the anxiety that accompanies the action. If you get overwhelmed, break down the emotions and tasks into smaller bits and do the very first thing on the list.

2. GUILT/SHAME. In order to improve on this emotion, it is essential to repair what has been broken. Guilt and shame generally result from an emotional response to acting in a bad way towards another person. Apologize and accept the consequences. As children we are afraid to confess or admit to having broken a window or object for fear of the consequences; more often than not the fear and anxiety itself was more intense than the punishment (unless you were

caught in a lie).

Commit to avoiding transgressions in the future and let it go. There is no benefit in worrying a bone that has been picked clean. The issue was resolved. Time to move on.

3. SADNESS. Move. Being active releases "feel-good" hormones. Do not avoid doing things because you are not up to it. The best remedy is to get up and move.

4. ANGER. GENTLY avoid the person that is causing you anger. Gently meaning as to not make it obvious or being passive aggressive about it. Attempt to empathize with the other person rather than blame.

What influences emotions?

Self-validation is an important part of understanding your inner-self, and a step required to regulate your behavior.

It is the process by which you reassure yourself that what you are feeling at that moment is real. It is important to you and it makes sense. A key thought to remember is that it is your own emotion, yes, it is valid, yes to you it is true but to others or in other types of situations it may not necessarily be readily acceptable.

Emotions are influenced by internal and external factors. They are also affected by certain things that are not a choice:

1. Cultural traditions and beliefs greatly affect how people express their emotions. Certain cultures find emotions and their expressions rude; in others, it is expected because not doing so is seen as being dishonest.

2. Genetics. The way our brains form in the womb is genetically determined. This is an aspect that we cannot control. We cannot change our genetics but although our brains are formed in a specific way due to this, they are able to be re-programmed.

3. Physical conditions of the brain and body such as tumors, Alzheimer's, metabolic

diseases will likely affect the person's emotional response to their specific situation.

Emotions are infectious in that when we see someone smile at us, our response is to mimic their behavior. This increases our emotional bond with that person, for example, you are greeted at the supermarket and the person smiles at you. Your Response is to smile back. The physical action of smiling affects your internal state. You feel a little bit happier after your encounter.

What we think impacts what we feel

We often take for granted exactly how interlinked our emotions and thoughts are. What you think will ultimately affect what you feel.

Thoughts will trigger emotions. If you are thinking about a big project that needs to be completed and you are worried about the timeline and ensuring the final product is up to the standard your boss requires, the worry will trigger fear. Thoughts and emotions have a profound effect on one another.

What is interesting is that *how* we approach the causes of our fears, affects how we feel.

As an example, a person with a fear of cats will approach their life in a way that either ensures that they do not encounter any cats in their day to day life. However, sometimes it may not be possible, so they will be hyper-aware of their surroundings; should a cat approach them they will automatically be on guard, expecting the worst because of their fear.

For a person who suffers no such difficulties, seeing a cat will have either a neutral or positive experience and response.

Can we change our thoughts and emotions?

In short, yes.

We are able to affect change by *altering* an external situation. We tend to think that some emotions are a part of life and are inevitable. Being in an unhappy relationship does not mean you need to stay in it. The emotions tied to that situation do not change unless you change them. You cannot force your partner to treat you differently, therefore, to extract yourself from that situation is the best way or alter the situation you are in and as a result the emotions tied to that situation.

We are able to affect change by *shifting* our focus from the negative aspect of the problem to something else that is more positive. Instead of thinking of how horrible the car accident was and how much paperwork is attached to the situation, shit your thoughts to the fact that no one was injured.

We are able to affect change by taking a second look and *re-appraising* a situation we find ourselves in. From the outset, we are focusing on the negative, "why is my boss constantly monitoring me? Do they not trust me to do my job"? Perhaps there are other, underlying reasons your boss may be monitoring you more often. By reevaluating the situation, you may notice instead that the boss is monitoring all other employees and not just you, or perhaps in earlier meetings, they may have mentioned the possibility of a promotion.

Some situations are not what they seem.

How we choose to live our lives has tremendous power over the way we feel every day. (Lawson, unknown)

Certain types of mental exercise and practice will affect our perceptions and views we have of the world. By practicing certain skills like journaling, mindfulness, and meditation you will feel calmer, more in control, and happier.

You will be more resilient in dealing with your responses when faced with difficult situations.

If you are aware of your thoughts and emotions, you are able to change them.

Identify

You are able to identify the sources of your troubles by being aware of what triggers the negative reaction.

Take a moment to notice any strong negative emotion you are experiencing or may have had experienced in the past. Just let your mind follow the motion. There is no reason for hostility towards yourself. Find that one moment in time where your emotional state shifted.

Like a switch that was flicked to the "on" position. When was it? What were you doing at the time?

Once you have located the moment the switch

happened, attempt to recall what it was about the situation had upset you. (Beck, 2014)

Did someone make a comment? Did you break your favorite mug?

Trying to locate the exact trigger may take some time as one event may only be overshadowing the other because you *already* feel upset. Making use of a journal to write down your thoughts in as much detail as possible, will certainly assist in this task.

To be fair, this is an exercise in hindsight. Most likely you will not recognize your negative thoughts and their causes in the moment (at least, not yet and not without practice).

Once that moment approaches, as your brain reacts to a situation and your reflexive response pops up, you will become aware of it. You will be able to change direction and diffuse the situation and negate the negative thoughts.

Chapter 4: Let's Set Goals

What is a goal?

A goal is a thing we aim for in life. It is our ambition and the ultimate target of our efforts.

How to Set a Goal

First, consider what you want to achieve. What is it you want to do? Where is it you want to be? Who do you want to be? What would you like to learn? These are some of the questions we often ask of young children.

"What do you want to be when you grow up?"

While you may think it a bit juvenile at first, the question is still very important. Not all goals need to be earth-shattering.

So, go ahead, ask yourself. You may be surprised by the answer.

And then commit to it.

Set SMART goals:

Specific - Be specific. Vague goals equal vague results.

Measurable - Instead of "one day" use dates or months. Or, quantities: I want to drink x amount of water a day.

Attainable - "I want to move to Japan next week" isn't really attainable. There is planning to be done and visas to get (which certainly wouldn't take a week).

Relevant - Relevant to you. Use _I_ phrases. _I_ want to travel. _I_ want to be healthier. You cannot force other people to fit in with your own goals. "I want my partner to propose by the end of the year." This one isn't up to you. Do not stress yourself out by creating a goal that is not fully in your hands.

Time-bound. Sometimes we set unrealistic goals in terms of timeframe _or_ we neglect to add a timeframe at all, thinking that we will reduce the stress attached to deadlines if we do so. Set lifetime goals first. Followed by shorter time frames such as the ten, five and two-year goals. Followed by monthly, weekly, and daily.

Having a solid list of what it is you wish to achieve makes them easier to track and easier to achieve. They give you a starting point and they motivate you.

Then go ahead and plan the steps you have to take in order to realize your goal. If your goal is to move to another country, list all the steps required to make it a reality. Each step is a small goal in itself - do not forget that! Smaller goals are what help you reach your lifetime goals.

There are many different genres of goals you can set for yourself. What you choose to set as a goal is up to you.

Below are some examples of categories you could make use of:

1. Career goals– Where do you want to be in your career? Do you want a change?

2. Financial goals– Do you have debt to pay off? Are you saving up for a specific goal?

3. Education– Do you want to go to school? Acquire a specific skill? How will you do that?

4. Familial goals– Do you want to start a

family? Do you need to add extra rooms for a growing family (this goal may be closely related to financial goals)?

5. Hobbies/artistically centered goals– Do you have a hobby you want to improve skills on? Do you want to turn a hobby into a business in the future?

6. Attitude adjustments– Are you acting in a way you disapprove of? Do you want to present as a friendlier person? How can you change this?

7. Health and fitness goals– Do you want to live a healthier life? Do you want to enter a fitness competition or run a marathon?

8. Giving back– How do you want to be able to give back to the world? Volunteer at a

shelter or soup kitchen? Donate money or clothing? If so, figure out how you would want to make the world a better place.

How can setting goals help?

Goals are the life force of success. Here are a few reasons why.

1. Goals provide you with direction.

2. Goals help illuminate your path, making it easier to know which changes you need to make in your life.

3. Goals provide motivation.

4. Goals help you believe in yourself.

5. Goals will assist you in pinpointing your true goals and eliminating distractions.

6. Goals help build self-confidence and help you to believe in yourself.

7. No matter how small a goal, achieving them is satisfying.

8. Breaking goals down into smaller ones makes the impossible suddenly seem possible.

9. Goals show you what it is you *truly* want.

Remember to keep this process going by marking off what you have achieved; reviewing what it is you felt before, during, and after achieving the goal. Update your goals if they seem to be more than you can handle:

Turn "I will drink 8 glasses of water a day" into "I will drink a glass each morning and sip from a bottle each day." By updating your goal, you have evaluated your successes and potential failures. You are managing your goals by regularly keeping track of how hard you can and are willing to push yourself without adding unnecessary risk of failure.

How can you monitor your progress as you go through CBT?

Evaluate and reflect

If you do not evaluate, how will you know if you are succeeding? Are you holding yourself accountable? Are you keeping track?

You can track things like mood and behavior using a tracking chart that you can create for yourself. The vertical axis will indicate mood from low to high. The horizontal axis will be the timeline i.e. days of the week.

You can use this chart to mark a dot on the scale to indicate how your mood was for the day. Is your mood improving? Keep in mind that it will most probably still fluctuate but is it better overall?

Are you working towards your goals? Are certain troubling behaviors, thoughts, and attitudes changing and improving? Are you actively working on these areas?

How to Tell Cognitive Behavioral Therapy is Working for You

There are a few ways you can evaluate if the program is working for you.

1. You have learned a new skill or two– A skill is an ability that utilizes the knowledge you have built up to perform a task optimally. Using a Mood Scale or Thought Journal to address and track your negative thoughts and emotions is considered a skill.

Being generally more positive is not a skill but a change of mindset instead.

2. You are making progress towards your long-term goals– A good way to evaluate effectiveness is how far you have come towards your long-term or lifetime goal.

3. You can see the results– This seems self-explanatory; however, do not neglect the

progress you make on the tasks you practice or the "homework" you are doing. Every little bit helps.

4. Other people notice results– Cognitive behavioral therapy helps you focus on achieving specific goals. When you have started to notice that you are reaching your goals, those around you will notice as well and share in your victories.

5. You have a new enthusiasm for reaching your goals– CBT is not about dwelling in the past or ancient emotions, it is about developing new skills that will arm you to move forward towards your goal and a happier, more satisfied life.

Success can only be measured by yourself and your inner realization that you are improving. This is why keeping record of your progress will help you see it sooner rather than later.

Potential obstacles that you face with cognitive behavioral therapy

As it is, cognitive behavioral therapy challenges you on a personal level. At times it will get tougher because of certain obstacles you may come across.

1. You may experience difficulty in identifying certain emotions. This is normal. Consider it as a way to relearn the different emotions, their triggers, and associated accepted behaviors.

In order to bridge this obstacle, instead of naming an emotion, you will start by narrowing down your thoughts first.

"What was your thought when x happened?"

"What did you tell yourself during x?"

"What did you do before x emotion/event happened?"

By doing this you get a grasp on the sequence of events that led to a specific emotion. This will help you identify said emotion in the future.

2. You know and understand the technical aspects of what is expected of you, but you just cannot bring yourself to act or incorporate them. Do not panic. This is generally an issue when you overthink certain things. The goal here is to

practice getting out of your own head and let your instincts guide you. Again, you may feel that your instincts are wrong but sometimes disconnecting from your mind is the best way to promote change. The key in this situation in practice and repetition.

3. You have low motivation. When you start feeling like continuing or actively participating is just a waste of time and energy or you are "just doing this to get that specific someone to stop nagging" this is the moment to focus on how cognitive behavioral therapy will benefit you in the long run.

You need to accept that there will be no one but yourself to hold you accountable. While you may decide to do a program like this with a friend or family member; the practice, the problem-solving and time put into achieving your goals, are ultimately your responsibility.

Focus on what you want out of cognitive behavioral therapy.

4. You will be afraid. Whether it is fear of change or unfamiliar situations or the laser-focus on your emotions and thoughts that make you uncomfortable, fear is part of the process. The trick is to face it. One small step at a time.

Identify your fears. Learn how to manage them and make use of your support system. You may be using CBT as an individual but having people around who support your willingness to change and who help keep you on track is often the weight that tips the scales towards success.

5. You do not believe in yourself.

This is a common obstacle. You may believe that you're not good enough. You may believe you do not deserve to change, or that you do not deserve the dreams you have set for yourself.

Pay attention to this negative inner voice and replace it. Encourage your friends and family to tell you whenever you give in to this self-doubt.

6. You feel overwhelmed.

All of this information is new to you. Think of starting cognitive behavioral therapy as organizing a messy bedroom.

This is a normal part of the process, even though you may feel like you would much rather just close the door and walk away.

What can you beforehand to prevent these obstacles from attaining your goal?

Accept that therapy is a work-in-progress.

You are not defined by your failures but how you deal with them.

Be prepared for setbacks.

Have a support structure set up when you start.

Be open-minded.

Remain consistent.

Be prepared to rewrite your goals several times.

Be prepared to accept that you cannot compare yourself to others doing the same therapy; people are not the same, problems are not the same. Therefore, progress will not be the same.

Achieving Goals

You have achieved a goal. Congratulations!

Now take the time to enjoy the satisfaction of having reached one of your goals.

Take the time to understand what that means: you are one step closer to your lifetime goal.

You succeeded. You did this.

Chapter 5: Identifying and Tackling Your Worst Nightmares

What is Anxiety?

Learning about Anxiety

Learning about a psychological problem can give you the background that will make addressing and overcoming the problem a lot more effective. Sometimes it could be beneficial to have close family and friends learn about your problem along with you. Having an understanding and social support during the process of working through and overcoming your problems can prove to be incredibly beneficial on the road to recovery. For example, a person who struggles with panic and anxiety attacks would begin by learning what anxiety is and what a panic attack is. In learning about these troublesome emotions and their physiological responses, they would come to understand that while uncomfortable and often terrifying, they are not dangerous or life-threatening.

The effects are temporary and can be controlled and reversed with practice.

Everyone experiences some form of anxiety and fear at one point or another. Whether it is before an exam or a job interview or pre-wedding jitters. Some anxiety in our daily lives is useful.

Anxiety helps us process and react appropriately to environmental stressors and threats, causing an increase in blood flow to the legs, quickening the heart rate and reflexes as a response and preparation for fight or flight– the feeling generally dissipates once the stressful situation has passed.

Anxiety becomes a problem when those feelings persist, they do not pass after an amount of time, they're extreme relative to the situation at hand, and they seem to be uncontrollable. When anxiety is severe enough it ends up interfering with our daily activities and causes difficulties in coping with and participating in daily life.

The feelings associated with anxiety are incredibly intense and disconcerting; they last for months and may vary in degrees of severity but never actually disappear. The emotions negatively affect your thoughts and increases stress levels which affect your health leaving you feeling distressed, pressured, and overwhelmed with life.

Anxiety causes physical symptoms that tend to be the person's main concerns; such as heart palpitations, dizziness, stomach cramps, and indigestion. It affects work performance and interpersonal relationships with friends, family, and coworkers.

It is also common for those who have anxiety to also feel depressed. It is important to note that these symptoms overlap, so be aware that should this be the case it does not necessarily mean that you suffer from depression as well.

Types of anxiety

Please note that the following list is not meant to be used as a diagnostic tool. Should you feel that you may have any of these disorders and symptoms it is advised to see a trained professional. However, these lists are to give you a general overview and insight into some of these disorders.

The most common are as follows:

Generalized Anxiety Disorder is when you worry about a various number of things, on most days for six or more months.

Phobias are extreme and irrational fears about a specific thing. A fairly common example is *agoraphobia*, often thought to be a fear of open spaces. It has been updated to include the fear of tight spaces, often going hand-in-hand with being away from safety- in the form of a loved one or a place that provides a feeling of comfort. Phobias are serious and often debilitating, causing sufferers to avoid leaving their homes in order to avoid the situations as described above.

Obsessive Compulsive Disorder is when you

have or experience unsolicited and intrusive thoughts or feelings that are uncontrollable in most cases. These feelings cause anxiety and fear which are only mediated by adapting behavior to ease the anxiety. While knowing that these thoughts are irrational, you may not be able to stop them. For example, the person may be afraid of germs and try to relieve the anxiety through repeated hand washing or sanitizing or avoiding touching things like handrails in the subway or shaking hands with people.

Panic Disorder is when you experience panic attacks. They can be classified as intense feelings of stress and anxiety that are projected in the form of physical symptoms. While not life-threatening these feelings and sensations are uncomfortable and make the sufferer feel like they may be dying. These symptoms include chest pains, breathing difficulties, heart palpitations, sweating, and shaking uncontrollably. These feelings and symptoms appear and disappear rapidly, aggravated by an environmental trigger and stressor.

What are the signs and symptoms?

Some common anxiety symptoms include:

1. hot and cold flashes

2. shaking uncontrollably

3. rapid heart rate, that is not related to physical exertion

4. tightness in your chest or chest pains

5. struggling to draw breath

6. your mind feeling like it is constantly racing

7. a constant and pressing desire to check up on things, to ensure that they are in working order or clean and tidy

8. persistent worrying about things that seem silly and unreasonable

People with anxiety disorders have recurring, intrusive and persistent thoughts and feelings that may cause them to avoid these situations that might cause concerns.

Possible causes include:

1. environmental stressors, such as workplace difficulties or personal issues with partners or family

2. medical factors, such as diseases or the effects of medications or the person having

been in prolonged surgery and recovery

3. withdrawal from an illicit substance. Often the withdrawal compounds the effects of other symptoms related to anxiety

What is Depression?

When a negative or distressing event happens in your life, for example, the passing of a close relative or the loss associated with a breakup, having feelings of sadness is pretty standard fare. Generally, over time, these feelings will diminish and go away or improve. However, in the event of depression, you feel a constant sadness or hopelessness and the feelings do not improve or go away even when the related factors improve.

The way you feel when you are depressed is

connected to:

1. your personal thoughts

2. your behavior

3. past events that still have bearing on you in the present such as a traumatic event

4. current events

5. the way your brain is wired to deal with the stress hormone cortisol

It is quite helpful to note that most depression will be helped or alleviated by practicing better self-care and utilizing self-help techniques that are designed to address these feelings, which include structured activity and planned or scheduled pleasurable activities.

Please be aware when these techniques are not

effective due to the severity of your condition it is advised that you seek the help of a medical professional. Turning to your support structure you have set up for yourself is also beneficial.

Needing help does not make you weak. It simply means that you still need to develop the skills in order to cope with these feelings.

Depression often leads to unwanted thoughts of inadequacy and worthlessness, believing that you are alone, and that the world would be better off without you in it.

What are the signs and symptoms?

The signs and symptoms of depression should be taken seriously, especially if they persist or do not improve for a length of time. Speak to your doctor should you feel unsafe at any time.

Key Signs

1. constant feelings of hopelessness and dysphoria

2. no longer having the energy or the desire to continue with activities that previously brought you pleasure and happiness.

Other things to watch out for

1. irritability and restlessness

2. lethargy and fatigue

3. feelings of emptiness and loneliness

4. disturbances in sleeping patterns, sleeping

more or less than is normal for you

5. losing or gaining weight

6. guilt and feelings of shame with regards to your previous actions

7. problems with concentration

8. reduced sex drive

9. consistent and obsessive thoughts about death

10. thoughts of harming yourself

It is also common for those who have depression to also feel anxious. It is important to note that these symptoms overlap, so be aware that should this be the case it does not necessarily mean that you suffer from anxiety as well, although the likeliness is good.

While depression may be the most common of the mental disorders, it is treatable, and you can live a relatively normal life between therapy and medication

Not everyone who is depressed experiences each symptom. Everybody is different and will experience symptoms in varying degrees, some experiencing more than others. The severity and frequency of symptoms and duration depend on each individual, their illness and the stage or severity of their condition.

Fear

Fear can be defined as an emotion that arises in response to an anticipated threat that triggers the flight or fight response, within the human brain, that was adapted for survival. The threat can be real or imagined, but the physical response is the same: elevated heart rate, rapid breathing, etc.

While fear is the emotional response associated with a perceived threat in our immediate environment, it can lead to freezing or withdrawing from the threatening situation.

Fear can be identified through physical sensations such as an increase in perspiration, sudden heart palpitations, dry throat and mouth, and the shaking of the limbs.

Additionally, these symptoms can oftentimes present with increased aggression if continually confronted with the fear-trigger.

Stress

"In a medical or biological context stress is a

physical, mental, or emotional factor that causes bodily or mental tension." (MedicineNet, 2018)

Stress is the physical counter-response to fear. When we are stressed, our body believes it is under threat and switches to 'fight or flight' mode. During this response, various chemicals are released into the brain in order to prepare the body for the physical action that is soon to follow. This causes a series of chemical and physical reactions within ourselves, from blood being diverted to muscles for the act of running away from danger (or towards it in some cases) to shutting down unnecessary bodily functions that use up the resources required elsewhere in the body during this stress-response. Such processes include digestion, which is why excessive stress causes a whole host of intestinal and digestive issues such as ulcers and stomach aches.

While this response proved useful when our ancestors faced dangerous predators, in our current modern existence, the constant stress response in our brains, due to the external triggers, ends up being harmful over a long period of time.

In our modern world, the 'fight or flight' response can still assist us in certain situations that could prove fatal if we do not respond quickly. Such situations include the split-second response required to slam on the brakes when someone runs in front of your car.

The challenge we face comes in when our body enters into a stress-response in situations that do not require it. Blood flow is redirected to muscles that are used for running (or fleeing), the brain functionality is greatly reduced.

This affects our ability to think straight, a stress-response that will negatively affect our work performance. If these conditions are maintained for long periods of time, our personal health is compromised; the results being elevated cortisol levels; increased blood pressure and respiratory issues.

Some of us avoid our stressors, removing or distancing ourselves from the situation or unpleasant event instead of tackling it. Called the survival instinct, inherent in all of us, that can save our lives in dire situations. However, in day to day life, this instinct can lead to a events and situations becoming progressively worse, increasing our stress levels when we realize that we are unable to solve the situation by running away.

A third effect the stress-response elicits is to freeze. Our joints and muscles lock up and we are unable to act or respond. This option is utilized when we are seemingly faced with an impossible choice and we feel that the only way out is to not react or choose at all. Holding our breath and shallow breathing are both forms of this response. Think of the characters in a scary movie, sometimes they will respond by freezing, holding their breath, or breathing shallowly. The occasional deep sigh is the nervous system catching up on its oxygen intake. (American Institute of Stress, 2018)

Cause and Effect

Many of the most popular and effective Cognitive Behavioral Therapy techniques are applied to what psychologists call "cognitive distortions" (Grohol, 2016).

Cognitive distortions are the inaccurate thoughts that you experience which reinforce negative thought patterns and emotions.

Cognitive distortions are the broken ways of thinking we have come to develop over the years that makes us believe in a reality that is different from the truth.

1.Filtering

Filtering refers to the way we ignore all of the positive and good things that occur in our day and focus only on the negative.

2. Polarized Thinking or "Black and White" Thinking

There is no gray area. It is an all or nothing manner of seeing things. If you fail at something it is seen as a total loss instead of a learning experience or an aspect of life that need to be worked on.

3. Overgeneralization

Overgeneralization is the act of taking one incident or event at any given point of time and using it as the only important point in order to draw a conclusion. For example, having one bad interview is seen as you are unsuccessful in all interviews and thus motivation to continue working towards acing the next interview gets diminished.

4. Jumping to Conclusions

This is similar to overgeneralization in that it involves having a faulty automatic response when drawing conclusions. Jumping to conclusions refers to the belief that something is absolute truth without any supporting evidence. You are convinced that your colleagues do not like you, regardless of them having never done or said anything to prove this point.

5. Catastrophizing

This involves expectations that the worst will happen despite having no supporting evidence or having the belief that the worst possible scenario is about to unfold. For example, as seen in a previous example, you may make a small mistake at work and be convinced that it will ruin the project you are working on, your boss will be completely furious, and you will lose your job as a result. Alternatively, we may minimize the importance of positive things in our lives, such as reaching a significant milestone in your career or having completed a difficult task.

6. Personalization

Often a distortion associated with Obsessive Compulsive Disorder in which the specific individual believes that they can control all the bad things around them and will adjust and adapt their behavior to accommodate for the increase in anxiety. They may believe that by not knocking on wood, bad luck was introduced and bad things happened. For example, should they have arrived later than planned to an event and things go bad during the event, i.e. someone started a fight, the person will believe that had they actually arrived on time, these things would not have happened.

7. Control Fallacies

Another distortion involves feeling that everything that happens to you is a result of external forces or due to your own actions. Sometimes what happens to us is due to forces we cannot control, and sometimes what happens is due to our actions, but the false thinking is in assuming that it is always one or the other. We may assume that the quality of our work is due to working with difficult people, or alternatively that every mistake someone else makes is due to something we did.

8. Fallacy of Fairness

Fairness is a concept we have all been concerned with at one point or another. Life is not fair, and should we decide to go looking for fairness to balance out the universe we will end up resenting and being unhappy with our experiences in life. Sometimes things will go our way, and sometimes they will not, regardless of how fair it may seem.

9. Blaming

When some event or experience in our lives did not go as we had expected or it went wrong, we sometimes explain it away by assigning blame elsewhere. Sometimes you may blame another for your actions and behaviors. We are responsible for our own actions. In the same way, we are not responsible for the choices other people make, they are not responsible for ours.

10. "Shoulds"

"Shoulds" govern our way of life nearly implicitly. We set rules for ourselves that we feel are socially appropriate. By adhering to these rules, we believe that we are good people or "responsible" if we stick to these constructs. When we break our own rules, we feel guilty. For example, we may have an unofficial rule that we are irresponsible if we spend money unwisely and on unnecessary things, we will end up feeling incredibly guilty when we spend the smallest amount on something we do not need.

11. Emotional Reasoning

"I feel it; therefore, it must be true." This is incorrect thinking because our thoughts are often shaped by a misconception we have to the world. For example, if we feel unattractive, the truth must be that we are unattractive. Our emotions are not indicative of the objective truth in the given situation. However, even being aware of this concept we may struggle with separating the truth from how we feel.

12. Fallacy of Change

This is the belief that our happiness and self-worth are tied in with other people and their thoughts and actions. We expect them to change in order to suit our needs and should they be unable to change or be unwilling, we believe that they do not want us to be happy. We are responsible for our own happiness.

13. Mislabeling

This way of thinking is an extreme form of generalizing. We take one or two separate beliefs and set them as standards or full truths that apply to everything in our lives and everything we or other people do and are responsible for. Mislabeling is specific to using exaggerated and emotionally charged language to create as much impact and credibility as possible. For example, stating that a woman cannot have a career and a family, as her family is more important. Suggesting that she is a bad mother and a bad person for choosing herself over her family.

14. Always Being Right

The fallacy here lies in the false belief that you are always right; that you are never wrong, and your word is gospel. Being wrong is completely unacceptable and being right is more important than others' feelings. Often being unable to admit to being wrong, can cause damage to relationships.

15. Heaven's Reward Fallacy

We expect that whatever we sacrifice or "give up" will be rewarded. We may label this as Karma, believing that Karma will reward our good deeds and punish the actions of bad people. Again, life is not fair, and the world does not work that way, causing within us anger, resentment, and bitterness when we do not receive what we feel we deserve.

Many tools and techniques found in Cognitive Behavioral Therapy are intended to address or reverse these distortions in order to create a more realistic view of the world and improve our interaction with it. [2]

HOW TO WORK THROUGH YOUR:

Depression

Cognitive behavioral therapy has been found in many cases to be effective in addressing and treating milder forms of depression. It is

---

[2] Positivepsychologyprogram.com

recommended that CBT be completed with a trained psychologist or psychiatrist in the event that depression is severe. Depending on the severity, treatment can take the standard six to eight weeks or in special cases, it can stretch to longer periods of time and treatment is adjusted to accommodate for the changes and special needs associated with this specific situation. However, in many cases, significant improvement can already be noted after ten to fifteen sessions.

Self-help and Coping

There are a number of things you can do to reduce the symptoms, the effect, and the severity of depression. With proper diagnosis, treatment, and care most people are able to overcome their depression and live normal lives.

In many instances, regular exercise has been recommended to increase the release of endorphins which will create positive emotions, feelings, and an improved mood.

Get enough good quality sleep. Sometimes we have a tendency to neglect the simplest of remedies. Sleep helps the brain work through the events of the day and helps the body recuperate. Sleep also helps de-stress us. If we are able to increase the quality of sleep and reduce the interference in our sleeping patterns, we increase our chance of success.

Combining these suggestions with a healthy diet and reducing the intake of alcohol and other depressants can reduce the symptoms and improve our quality of life.

Depression is a serious condition. Please check in

with a therapist, doctor, or support group if you are experiencing distressing symptoms or experiencing a lapse in your progress.

Anxiety

Self-treatment

In some cases, a person can treat anxiety at home without the intervention of clinical supervision. Please be aware that this course of action may not be recommended or effective in instances where the anxiety is severe.

There are several exercises and actions to help you cope with anxiety:

1. Stress management: Reduce and limit potential triggers. Be organized. Plan ahead and have windows of time set aside

for yourself.

2. Relaxation techniques: These techniques include meditation, breathing exercises, self-care - in the form of relaxing, long baths, resting (but not sleeping) in a dark room to eliminate light stressors, and yoga.

3. Exercises to replace negative thoughts: Make a list of the negative thoughts that you are experiencing. Write down a second list with positive and believable thoughts. Visualizing these thoughts is beneficial.

4. Support network: Talk with people closest to you who support you. There are also support networks outside of your

immediate environment that can provide useful.

5. Exercise: Physical exercise (combined with a healthy approach to food) will improve your self-confidence, self-image and will release chemicals in the brain that trigger the positive emotions that help alleviate the symptoms of anxiety.

Counseling

A standard and widely accepted way of treating anxiety is through counseling and various therapies, which often include a combination of both psychotherapy and cognitive behavioral therapy. These therapies are often adapted to the client's specific needs, which is discussed with their chosen or assigned therapist.

Cognitive Behavioral Therapy

This type of therapy aims to change harmful thought patterns and actions that have formed the basis of anxious and troubled feelings. During this process, users of this form of therapy hope to eliminate or reduce the distorted ways of thinking and then change the way they react to places, objects, and situations that trigger episodes of anxiety.

For example, a practitioner treating a client for a panic disorder will attempt to reinforce that the feelings associated with panic attacks are not true heart attacks but exist only within the bounds of the anxious feeling. Repetitive exposure to fears and relative triggers is sometimes chosen as a technique to assist with therapy. This technique encourages people to confront their fears. Over longer periods of exposure, this can reduce their sensitivity to certain triggers which in turn assists in advancing healing.

The first step in exposure as a technique involves making an extensive list of situations, places, objects, and (rarely) emotions that you fear.

For example, to overcome your fear of snakes or spiders in order to enjoy more outdoor activities with your partner, your list would look something like this: looking at pictures of these two creatures, watching videos or clips featuring these fears, visiting a zoo or reptile house or aquarium in order to see them up close, and standing in the same room as someone handling a spider or snake. Once your list is complete you will rank them from least scary to scariest.

Now you can see where to start in order to overcome your fear. Start small and work your way up the list gradually. Approach the situation as you would training for a marathon: you do not just show up on the day and have at it. There is a lot of preparation involved.

A lot of what happens in cognitive behavioral therapy will follow a similar "training" regime.

Fear

Fear can be debilitating but it need not be. Below are some hints and tips in order to manage your fear and take a step back from the situation so you can assess.

1. Take a time out: It is impossible to think clearly when your brain is flooded with fear or anxiety. Forcing the situation causes the situation to escalate. Focus on taking a step back to evaluate. Take a breather and focus on calming yourself and your mind before getting back into the situation.

Distract yourself with a short walk, a cup of tea, or a quick session of meditation.

2. Breathe through it: Another method, if you are unable to calm yourself, is to ride it out. Breathe through the panic. Your heart rate will undoubtedly increase, and your body will respond in a physiological way that is appropriate for the emotional stimulation.

It is best not to fight the emotion or the accompanying physical response. Simply feel the panic and the fear without an attempt at distracting yourself. The goal here is to help the body get used to the sensations and to help it cope with them. Place a free hand on our stomach and just let it rest there, allow yourself to feel your stomach expand with each breath. Keep breathing through.

3. Face your fears: Avoiding them makes your perception of them worse. Face them, acclimatize and soon the negative feeling associated will start to disappear. If you experience a minor lapse in doing this exercise, accept that you are done for the day but try again tomorrow. Never give up.

4. Worst-case scenario: Try to imagine the worst of the situation at hand and play it out. There is a section where I go into more detail.

If you add logic into the equation, the size of the fear diminishes.

5. Look at the evidence: Take your fear and be realistic. You are afraid of the potential pain a spider bite can inflict, along with the added bonus of it being an enormous variant. Have you experienced a situation like this? Do you know of someone who has? What would your advice be to a friend suffering the same trigger and fear?

6. Do not try to be perfect: Life is stressful enough as it is without needing to compare yourself to

others or have this preconceived notion that everything you do must be perfect. It is simply not possible. Be the best you that you can be. There will be setbacks but do not let them dictate your progress. Try again.

7. Visualize a happy place: When we are overwhelmed by fear and anxiety, it becomes increasingly difficult to think of a happy thought. When you are taking a moment to calm your mind, use the opportunity to create a visual image of your happy place or recall a happy memory.

Allow the positive emotions wash over you.

8. Talk about it: If you cannot talk to your friends, family, or partner make contact with a help-line.

Some are available 24 hours a day.

Oftentimes all you have to do is talk about it. When you verbalize out loud what it is you are afraid of, ninety percent of the time you will realize that these fears are mostly unfounded.

The other ten percent you can deal with once you have identified them.

Small steps.

9. Go back to basics: Do not reach for caffeine or alcohol in order to help you cope. Return to basics. Sleep early, reduce light pollution in your bedroom, avoid using your phone right before bed, and eat a healthy home cooked meal instead of fast food.

A short walk and some sunlight are just what the

doctor ordered.

10. Reward yourself! Do not neglect yourself or minimize your accomplishments. Allow yourself a treat. Enjoy a small victory with a reward that will not set you back. Whether it is a walk outside or a visit to the countryside, a book, or that new pair of earrings you have been eyeing all week, do what makes you happy. Just keep in mind that these treats should not compromise the work you have put in.

Stress

Everyone—adults, teens, and even children—experiences stress at times. Stress can be beneficial. It can help people develop the skills they need to deal with possible threatening situations throughout life. Stress is not helpful when it prevents a person from taking care of themselves or their family. You can put problems into perspective by finding healthy ways to cope. Getting the right care and support can help reduce stressful feelings and symptoms.

Common reactions of stress

Common reactions include in any combination the following:

1. Disbelief

2. Shock and numbness

3. Feelings of helplessness and frustration

4. Fear about the uncertainty of the future

5. Guilt

6. Shame

7. Anger, tension, and irritability

8. Poor concentration

9. Procrastination

10. Crying

11. Reduced interest in usual activities

12. Wanting to be alone

13. Loss of appetite

14. Disturbed sleep patterns, in the form of either sleeping too much or too little

15. Nightmares or sudden recurring unpleasant memories

16. Replaying the event

17. Headaches, back pains, and stomach

aches, ulcers and digestive distress

18. Increased heart rate and difficulty breathing

19. Sudden use of cigarettes, alcohol or drugs; abuse of these substances

Healthy Ways to Cope with Stress

Feeling emotional, nervous, having trouble falling or staying asleep, as well as eating disturbances - i.e. eating too much or too little - is normal during times of stress; however, they are generally not the healthiest approach.

Below are some healthier options to cope with stress.

1. Take care of yourself

2. Eat healthy but balanced

3. Implement a healthy exercise regime

4. Get enough sleep

5. Take a break if you feel the pressures of stress

6. Share your problems and concerns with a support structure. Share how you are feeling and coping with the stresses in your life with either a parent, friend, counselor, doctor, or pastor.

7. Avoid drugs and alcohol and other stimulants. Initially these may seem to help you deal with stress but in the long run, these may cause you to become dependent and create additional issues that will only increase the stresses and

triggers you are already experiencing.

8. Grab some distance. If current news or events are causing you distress, you should take a break from these triggers and distance yourself from the things that cause the feelings of stress and anxiety.

Tips and tricks

Effective stress management assists in providing you with the tools needed to break the iron grip stress has on your life. This will ultimately help you be happier, healthier, and enjoy a more balanced life. You will be more productive and be able to have time for yourself and the things you love doing.

More importantly by practicing these techniques and applying them to your everyday life, you create the opportunity to embrace and challenge other potential stressors head-on.

However, it is important that you find the combination of techniques and other tips and tricks that will work best for you. What works for one person would not necessarily work for you.

Keep track of what you have tried and how it has affected your problems and how successful the challenges were dealt with during this process. The following tips may help you do that.

1: Identify the source

Stress management starts with identifying the sources of stress in your life. While it sounds like a pretty straightforward concept, pinpointing sources of *chronic* or recurring stress is much more complex and can very easily be overlooked or overshadowed.

The impact your own thoughts, feelings, and behaviors have on your everyday stress levels are often kept in the background by other, bigger stress triggers such as losing your job or moving to a new house. You may be aware that you are constantly worried about meeting work deadlines but consider instead that it is procrastination that is causing the added stress, rather than the high demands of your job.

Identify true sources of stress:

1. Is everything explained away as "just temporary" even though you cannot quite remember the feeling of *not* being anxious or stressed out?

2. Is stress in your home and work life seen as

"part of the routine"? Is it being dismissed as an integral part of the day to day running and no second thought is given?

3. Do you shift blame? Do you feel that the cause of your stress lies with others? Or that it is normal and par for course?

Until you accept responsibility for your own actions in and the role you play in creating stress it will always remain outside of your control.

Start a stress journal

In your journal, write down the following:

1. What has caused your stress (it can be as simple as being late for work, or having an unpleasant encounter with a clerk at the bank; take a guess if you are unsure)

2. How you felt, both physically and

emotionally

3. How you acted in response to the stress

4. And what you did to make yourself feel better, or what you did to help yourself overcome the emotion.

A stress journal is an excellent way to keep track and monitor the stressors in your life. By doing so, you are able to deal with them more effectively. Whenever you feel stressed, keep track of it in your journal.

You will begin to see patterns emerge from the perceived chaos and you will notice common themes.

2: Four A's of stress management

Given that stress is an automatic response by your nervous system, some stressors often arise at predictable and consistent times. These can include your commute to work and family gatherings, for example.

When dealing with such predictable stressors, you can either choose to change the situation or you can choose to change your reaction. When deciding on which path to take, keep in mind the four A's in dealing with stress: avoid, alter, adapt, or accept.

You are able to choose between these four actions either individually or in conjunction with one another.

1. Avoid unnecessary stress

It is not healthy to avoid a stressful situation in your day to day life, especially considering that the situation needs to be addressed in order to resolve it.

Learn how to say no.

Know what your limits are and set boundaries. Stick to your boundaries.

Whether in a personal or professional situation, taking on more than you can handle is a guaranteed way to induce stress. Avoid people who stress you out. You know who they are. If someone is consistently causing you stress in your life, limit the amount of time you spend with them.

Take control of your environment to create a workaround for the triggers that incite stress. If traffic makes you tense, take a scenic route to your destination.

Analyze your schedule. If you have too much on your plate, move tasks that are not essential or important to the bottom of your list or eliminate them entirely should they turn out to be unnecessary.

2. Alter the situation!

If you cannot avoid a stressful situation, attempt to alter it.

If something or someone is bothering you, tell them. Certainly, there are means and ways to say this to avoid coming across as being rude, if that is one of your concerns.

Be assertive and communicate.

Be willing to compromise. When requesting someone change their behavior or habits, be willing to do the same. Both parties need to be willing to bend in order to reach a happy middle ground.

Create a balanced schedule for yourself. "All work and no play" are by far the quickest route to burnout.

3. Adapt

If you cannot avoid or change the trigger, change yourself. You are made to adapt to stressful situations.

Regain control by subverting or changing what it is you expect.

Reframe problems and review stressful situations in a positive light. Change your perspective; instead of getting aggravated, irritated, or stressed out about being stuck in a traffic jam; see it as a unique opportunity to enjoy your own company and the solitude. Use the time to reflect.

Take a look at the big picture. How will this event or situation really affect you in the long run? Will it still have an impact tomorrow? In a week? A month? A year? Is it really worth it to get upset over the situation?

Adjust your standards. Set reasonable standards for yourself. Aiming for perfection will bring you nothing but a source of avoidable stress. Do not set yourself up to fail.

Practice gratitude. When stress is a major factor in your day to the point where it causes an extreme negative emotion, take a moment to think back on each small thing in your life that you value and appreciate - do not forget to include yourself in this. You have our own unique gift and qualities. This simple strategy can help you keep things in perspective.

4. Accept the things you cannot change

Some sources of stress are unavoidable. There are some events that will occur in your lifetime that are unavoidable. You cannot prevent the death of a loved one. In cases such as this, the best way to deal and cope with the associated stress is to accept the situation as is.

Do not attempt to control that which is uncontrollable. There are a host of things in life that we simply cannot control, for example, the actions of others. Instead of allowing these things to stress you out, focus instead on how you react to these situations.

Look on the bright side. When faced with the major challenges and their associated negativity, try to look at them as opportunities for personal growth. If it was your own actions that resulted in a stressful situation, look back and analyze them in order to learn from them.

Forgive. Accept that life is not fair nor is it perfect. People will, from time to time, make mistakes that negatively affect us on a personal level. Let go of anger and resentment. Forgive and move on. Spend your energy wisely.

Expressing what you are going through or experiencing. Opening up in this area will prove beneficial. Oftentimes just talking to someone can help ease the stress associated with a stressful event.

Having someone who cares about your well-being willing to listen even if there is nothing they can do to help, will bring you an irreplaceable sense of belonging.

3: Move

Physical activity relieves stress. Strenuous physical activity does not need to be in your routine in order for you to reap the benefits of getting up and moving.

Exercise releases endorphins that in turn make you feel good. The better you feel, the more you want to move and on and on. Being physically active also has the added benefit of being a good distraction for your anxieties.

While you will get the most benefit from regular activity for at least 30 minutes a day, it is perfectly reasonable to slowly build up your fitness levels in order to enjoy the experience more.

Do not disregard even the smallest amount of activity that you do. These little bursts of movement add up over the course of the day.

Get moving.

Below are some basic activities that you can add into your daily schedule:

1. Put on some music and dance around. Jiggle and wiggle. No one is watching. You shouldn't care about what others may think.

2. Take a walk with your dog

3. Walk or cycle to the store, instead of driving. Not only will you save a little on gas, but you will also be increasing your

fitness and mental health

4. Use the stairs at home or work, rather than an elevator

5. Park your car in the farthest spot in the lot and walk the rest of the way

6. Get a partner to help hold you accountable. Sometimes we drop exercise simply because doing it alone is no fun

Rhythmic Exercise

Choose an activity that you will love; this increases the odds of sticking with it until the end. While just about any form of physical activity can help burn away the tension and stress, rhythmic activities are particularly effective.

Good choices include walking, running, swimming, and dancing

During your activity, take careful note of how your body is responding alongside your movements. Add a small mindfulness element to increase success and break free of the cycle of negative thoughts.

4: Connect

It is important to note that the people you spend your time with cannot "fix" your problem. They are simply there to listen. Do be mindful of the additional aspect of looking weak. These people are your friends. You trust them and the people who care about you will not see it in a negative way.

On the contrary, this closeness will strengthen your bond.

Spending some quality time with trusted friends

or loved one's triggers feelings of safety and love. These in turn trigger hormones to release that naturally counteract the hormone linked to stress.

Of course, it is not always possible or realistic to have your closest friends available when you need them. This is why having a larger support network that you will be able to lean on will help you develop great resilience to life's setbacks.

Tips for building relationships

1. Help someone else

2. Become a volunteer

3. Have coffee with a friend

4. Ask a loved one to check in with you daily

5. Accompany someone to the movies

6. Get in contact with an old friend

7. Go for a walk with your workout buddy

8. Schedule a date once a week. It can be with a friend or your partner or even a potential partner.

9. Meet new people through hobbies

5: Schedule time for fun and relaxation

Carve out "me" time. Do not neglect yourself in the process of working through your problems. Schedule time for yourself. Self-care is a necessity.

Set aside a moment for leisure.

Include rest and relaxation in your daily schedule.

Just as you would not let your relaxation time or leisure time interfere with work obligations, likewise do not allow work or other obligations to interfere with your personal time. This time is specifically scheduled for you to enjoy a moment of respite, to recharge and relax your mind away from the distractions of everyday life.

Make it something you enjoy; add it to your schedule every day.

Keep your sense of humor. Laugh, whether it is at yourself or some funny event or action. Just do it. Laughter releases endorphins which stabilize and elevate your mood. It also assists the body in fighting off stress and stress-related illness.

Take up a relaxation practice such as yoga or meditation or relaxed breathing. These techniques trigger the body's calming response.

As you become more familiar with the techniques and the practice, your stress levels will decrease. Your mind and body will become calm.

6: Improve your Time Management Skills

Poor time management causes stress. Procrastination causes stress.

By putting off tasks that we find unpleasant or boring, we end up creating a bigger problem in the future.

When you are stretched thin, running behind, and stressed out because of various other reasons it is hard to stay calm and focused. The additional stressor in this situation is to reach for a creature comfort - more often than not these comforts are part of previous, unhealthy, and unhelpful habits that you have cultivated for the sole purpose of dealing with stress in the first place.

Focus on the things you can do instead:

1. Do not over-commit. Do not cause yourself

to be stretched too thin. Try not scheduling tasks or meetings back to back. Leave wiggle room to compensate for the possibility of something taking longer than anticipated.

2. Prioritize tasks. Make a to-do list. Tackle them in order of importance. Do the high-priority items first. Do not leave the most unpleasant for last. Do those first, then you will look forward to the easier, more pleasant tasks that lie ahead.

3. Break projects into smaller pieces. Often, we are overwhelmed by large projects that seem impossible and daunting. Break the bigger project up into smaller, more manageable ones.

4. Delegate responsibility. You do not have to

do it all by yourself. Share the responsibilities. If others are capable of taking over certain tasks from you - let them. Let go of control.

7: Maintain balance

In addition to regular exercise, you should incorporate other healthy lifestyle choices that could ultimately improve your resilience and resistance to stress.

Eat healthily. You need not necessarily go *on* a diet, the outcome we are aiming for is to reduce the amount of toxic substances we ingest. If your body is well-nourished you are better equipped to fight off stress and illness. Choose healthier options and try to eat balanced meals.

Reduce your caffeine and sugar intake. The

temporary high brought on by caffeine and sugar often ends with a massive dip in energy and mood; causing us to consume more in order to compensate for a sudden lack of energy and alertness.

Avoid alcohol, cigarettes, and drugs. These may provide a short reprieve from stress, but it will aggravate your symptoms when withdrawal kicks in.

Get plenty of sleep. Sleep assists the body and brain to reset.

8: Quick Stress Relief

Quick stress relief is exactly as advertised. Sometimes events happen out of the blue that trigger unforeseen bouts of stress and anxiety, for example having an argument with your partner before work.

The quickest way to reduce stress is by taking a deep breath.

Follow up each breath by activating your senses. Ground yourself in the moment. What do you see, what do you hear and smell and taste?

You can opt for a soothing movement instead, perhaps it is caressing the pendant around your neck that was gifted to you by your grandparents.

You could also focus on a photo, a piece of music.

By using these quick relaxation techniques, you can quickly ground yourself, relax, and focus.

The key is to experiment with different techniques and objects; discover the sensory experience or item that is unique to you and your needs. [3]

---

[3] https://www.helpguide.org/articles/stress/stress-management.htm/

Chapter 6: Stay on Track

How to Prevent a Relapse

Lapses will happen. You will feel pressured to succeed, you will feel stress and anxiety. You will experience a host of negative emotions. How you think about this setback plays a large role in your future thoughts and behavior. If you believe yourself to be a failure, you are more inclined to discontinue treatment which in turn causes a relapse.

No matter how badly you feel you messed up, you can never unlearn the skills required to deal with your problems; there may exist a temporary lapse in judgment which causes you to question yourself.

In order to manage your problems optimally, you

need to make practicing helpful skills a habit.

A *relapse* is a full return to your previous habits. A *lapse* is canceling on a friend because the stress of being with other people may be a bit much that day. However, you get right back into it.

A *relapse* is feeling "I already messed up, there is no point in restarting" and then canceling all plans and giving up altogether.

Here are some tips on how to prevent a lapse from turning into a relapse:

1. Practice. Keep practicing the skills you are learning during your therapy.

2. Set a schedule for practice

3. Be aware of triggers that could cause you to have a lapse- have a list of "warning signs" that a lapse is imminent.

4. Have an action plan to deal with these triggers

If you experience a lapse, do not beat yourself up but rather try to learn from it. What was the situation preceding the lapse? What were your thoughts and emotions? Breaking it down in this manner, you will have a more accurate understanding of the things that cause a lapse and you can then create a more detailed plan to help cope with future difficulties.

5. Hold yourself accountable but,

6. Be kind to yourself. A lapse does not mean failure! It means the program needs adjusting.

Additionally, by identifying your problem and then progressively working on solutions to these problems, whether by yourself or with a trusted friend can help ease negative feelings and thoughts. For example, you could meet up with people who share similar interests with you and spend some time to connect.

Learn to write positive self-statements to counteract your negative thoughts.

After you have located the root cause of your negative thinking, write down each negative thought you use to rebut any positive one that might arise. Write a self-statement to counteract each negative thought.

Remember and repeat these self-statements back to yourself whenever you start to notice the return of a negative thought. Given time, you will be readjusting your thinking and the negativity will be replaced by the positive thought structures.

The self-statement should not be too far from the

negative thought or be presented as an overly positive statement as your mind might not accept it.

For example, if the negative thought, "I'm so stupid," is replaced by one that could be seen as outlandish to yourself, "I'm really smart," a better statement could be, "I could certainly improve in certain skills that could make me feel less stupid."

The message here is that it is okay to be positive about yourself and your situation, but you need to keep it in check to avoid disappointment, especially early on in therapy when you are still vulnerable to small changes in thinking that could cause a setback. (Anderson, 2014)

Create new opportunities for yourself in which to feel positive emotions.

If you meet a new person and you immediately think that their laugh is annoying; create the opportunity to retrain your thinking by instead coming up with five things that you *do* like about them.

"Carmichael recommends "buddying up" with someone else working on the same technique. That way, you and your buddy can get excited over having positive thoughts and experiences to share with each other throughout the day." (Anderson, 2014)

At the end of each day, during a moment of reflection, write down the events that happened in your life that day that you are appreciative or thankful of.

Learn to accept that disappointment is a normal part of life. Often failure is seen in a completely negative light. The situations that result in disappointment are inevitable, it is *how* you choose to deal with and respond that will determine how soon after you can get back on track again.

Remember that certain things are out of your control and you should not feel negative about the things you cannot change.

Work on what *is* in your control. Utilize your journal. Write down the situation, identify the negative emotions, the resulting actions, and how the situation has taught you some new lessons.

Take the time to determine how you would be able to approach a similar situation next time to improve on it and possibly have it turn out a success. These exercises will help improve your mood and your outlook on your future.

Prevent Yourself from Deflecting your Goals

Key techniques to Avoid Deflection or Procrastination

Relaxation Strategies

Learning how to relax is an essential part of therapy, especially when the situation becomes intense. Tension and incorrect breathing are linked to stress and anxiety. It is important to be aware of what your body is telling you.

It may seem like a simple thing, but many people neglect this step, opting to "push through".

The goal, however, of relaxation is not to procrastinate or put off what needs to be done. The techniques are used to alleviate the symptoms of anxiety and stress to help you manage your problems and reach your goals.

Often there are two very simple, very common techniques associated with cognitive behavioral therapy:

1. Calm breathing

2. Progressive muscle relaxation.

The more these are practiced, the more effective they become. Sometimes these techniques are combined with other practices such as yoga, meditation, and mindful journaling.

How to work around procrastination

Procrastination is a coping mechanism. We often put off tasks that make us feel anxious, sometimes it is an important or urgent task that we set aside in favor of a lighter or easier one simply because of dreading tackling the bigger one.

This does not mean you are lazy. You are simply responding to the emotional response that the task elicits: anxiety.

With the help of cognitive behavior therapy, you will be able to recognize and acknowledge these emotions that cause you to behave in a certain way.

Here are five ways you can pull away from procrastinating and getting right back into moving forward with goals and tasks that will, ultimately, reduce long-term stresses.

1. Recognize that you are, indeed, procrastinating. This can be hard to spot

sometimes, especially if you are actually getting things done, just not what *must* be done. You could be prioritizing smaller tasks. Even something as simple as starting a big project but getting up to make a cup of tea or getting a soda. "Preparing" to start, i.e. doing anything *but* actually sitting down to work.

2. Ask yourself why? Why are you procrastinating? Oftentimes it is a sense of being overwhelmed or doubting your skills to complete the task at hand.

3. Commit. You may have deviated in the past and procrastinated in the past but take action now and stick to what you are doing.

4. Start with the least enjoyable tasks first. You may be tempted to go for the easier

tasks and leave the others for later but tackle the more unpleasant ones first thing in the day so that you have something more enjoyable to look forward to.

5. Set up a plan to keep you on track. Ask someone to check in on you to hold you accountable. Reward yourself.

Bonus tip: **Minimize distraction**. It is easy to give in to other things that end up distracting us and pulling us away from important objectives. By minimizing distraction, you increase the chance of success. The hardest part of any task is getting started. This holds even more truth when it comes to needing to do unpleasant tasks.

Maintain Your Goals

Goals are what will help you measure how successful cognitive behavioral therapy is for you. Keep track of them, update them, and be proud of what you have accomplished thus far.

Take additional Preventive Measures

There are also other ways we overlook at which we can reduce the feelings of stress and anxiety and reduce the effect certain triggers will have on your mental state. Anxiety does not equal a mental disorder unless it severely affects your day to day functioning.

However, even in a normal setting certain thing can aggravate feelings of anxiousness.

1. Reduce your intake of drinks that contain

caffeine.

2. Reduce the intake of sugar.

3. Maintain a balanced diet.

4. Nix the medications (if at all possible) or if you are trying to switch to an herbal alternative, check in with your care physician to ensure these won't have an adverse effect.

5. Create a regular sleeping pattern and stick to it. Avoid using your phone or other devices before bed.

6. Avoid alcohol and other recreational substances. While you may feel these are helping your current mood or keeping your anxiety in check, they are not long-term solutions and may end up causing

more damage or creating a secondary
dependency.

Chapter 7: Quick Exercises for You

Realistic Thinking

Thoughts affect our emotions, therefore identifying and replacing negative thoughts with more tempered ones.

Realistic thinking requires the adjustment of negative thoughts into *neutral* thoughts. By being neither negative or too positive you create a balanced view and frame of reference with which to work while progressing through cognitive behavioral therapy.

An example:

Negative thinking is reflected as follows, "I am bad at presentations." A modified version that impacts and adds to the negativity could read, "I am the worst at presentations." Not only are you thinking negatively about your own skill set, you are immediately comparing it with others.

A positive thought could be: "I am the best at presentations." or "I am better than Susan at presentations."

In this instance, you could feel as though you are lying in order to not be negative. Alternatively, being overly positive may lead to a negative rebound later in the day when your presentation does not go as well as you had hoped.

Be truthful with yourself.

Instead, a muted approach is better. "I am not as good as I could be at presentations. I will practice more and ask other people for advice."

In this example you have created an expectation

of yourself that is not overly critical, nor is it bordering on a falsehood that could create additional anxiety.

Steps to Realistic Thinking

1. Be aware of your thoughts.

2. Identify the thoughts that cause unreasonable negativity. Being sad because you lost a parent is normal. Being sad because you feel "nobody likes me" is an unrealistic thought.

3. Be aware of even the smallest emotional shift

4. Ask questions, challenge your thinking. Are any of these thoughts based in truth?

5. Come up with an alternative thought to replace the negative one.

You can also make use of "coping statements" that will unconsciously provide you with a little motivation. For example, you may be feeling extremely anxious about doing a big presentation at work. You can encourage yourself by reminding yourself that you have succeeded before and you are capable of succeeding again.

Make use of positive self-statements.

 "I am capable."

"I am qualified."

"I am good at my job."

Essential Techniques in CBT

Sometimes we need a guiding hand in what exactly we can do to make cognitive behavioral therapy work for us.

Journaling

"Dear diary···"

There is a reason journaling is introduced as a first exercise. It allows you to see your thoughts in physical form and so become more aware of them and their effect on your life. Write about your day to day experiences and events. With this technique, you should keep track of your mood. You can be as creative as you want to make the experience more enjoyable. Draw a smiley face instead of writing down a word for how you feel.

The aim is to keep track of your emotions,

thoughts, and associated behaviors. With time you will be able to accurately intercept them in your day to day activities and learn how to change or adapt them.

Mood Scale

Keep track of your moods on a chart. As explained previously, use the vertical axis to indicate your mood from low to high and the horizontal axis as the timeline i.e. days of the week or should you wish to be more specific, hours of the day.

You could also modify this to include your mood before, during, and after activities to help you focus on the things that would cause you the most distress.

Thought Restructuring

This is the act of taking an automatic thought that you have identified as being negative or harmful and pull it apart to find out *how* this thought came to be, you will begin to learn all about this specific thought.

Where it came from.

Why do you believe it?

When you find a thought or belief that is harmful, you will challenge yourself by asking "is this belief really true?"

For instance, if you believe that in order to be happy you need to advance quickly in your career, but it doesn't seem to happen, you will begin believing that there may be something wrong with you and will start to become unhappy.

You do not accept the negative thought but think of other ways you can be happy. You will challenge your own self-destructive belief.

Is advancement really going to make me happy or is that just what I think?

List other ways you could possibly be happy in your career without the need for advancement. You could focus instead on being the best at what you do, regardless.

Interoceptive Exposure

Interoceptive refers to the sensations *inside the body*, such as the "butterflies" we feel when anxious.

This technique is aimed at the feelings of anxiety and panic attacks - tight chests, heart palpitations, etc.

Expose yourself to these sensations without avoiding them.

The aim here is to feel the sensations as they are. They are not dangerous.

Scary, yes, but not harmful.

Feelings of panic tend to compound one another, meaning they are linked and affect one another in a sort of cyclical way. If you are afraid of having a panic attack you will most likely trigger one.

Play the Scenario

Sometimes we like to imagine future outcomes. For people who have a tendency to overthink, the point of this exercise is to play through the whole scenario.

Sometimes you would stop at what you consider a "bad" part and recoil from the fear and anxiety it stirs up, pushing the thought away but it is still at the back of your mind. Which, in its own way, will aggravate anxiety and fear because you do not resolve the outcome of that scenario. It remains as a "what if".

Visualize your fear and realize that even should all the bad things you are imagining happen, you will be okay.

We are programmed to think of worst-case scenarios; it is how we adapted and evolved. Without this fear response to our environment, we would likely have died out.

The purpose is not to give in to the fear but to

accept that the outcomes we imagine rarely come to fruition.

As an example, I have a big meeting with my boss in the morning about one of the projects I am working on. He gave no topic of discussion, so in my mind I am over analyzing everything I have done on the project and every step I reported to him, imagining that at some point I may have done something that he did not like. Perhaps the client is unhappy with the progress.

Perhaps I may end up being pulled from the project or risk losing my job.

In each of these instances, I am imagining the worst things that can happen, but I do not go further than the negative outcome possibilities.

This leaves me tense and anxious which can

translate into physical symptoms as well: upset stomach, heart palpitations, cold sweats, headaches, and sleeplessness which in turn worsens the anxiety I already feel.

These symptoms have a negative effect as well, causing me to believe that something really will go wrong.

Take it a step further. I play out each scenario until the very end:

I did a bad job, I am removed from the project and all future projects because I believe that this project is one that would have made my career. Let us assume that I will also lose my job because of the high-profile nature of this particular project.

Now what?

I am unemployed. I have received my severance package. I take a couple of days to regroup my thoughts and analyze the situation. I do not dwell long in the negativity, but I decide that now is the time to focus on starting my own business like I had wanted to since college but took that job because it was what was expected of me.

When in actuality the scenario would probably play out a little closer to this: the next morning when it is time for our meeting together, I learn he has called me in just to touch base and to provide guidance, even assistance. I return to my desk feeling drained because of the stressful night. Nothing bad had happened after all.

Take note how the thought pattern changes along the way; from anxiety fueled chaos, it turns to calculated, neutral thoughts of where to go next.

Play through your own scenarios until the end.

The following are a couple of things to keep in mind and to utilize while doing this exercise. These points will help you strip down your fears into malleable and manageable chunks:

1. Identify what you are most afraid of in the scenario. Be specific and very detailed. Ask yourself the true likelihood of this event happening.

Once you have identified the perceived negative outcome or threat, rate it on a scale of one through ten, the likeliness of this actually coming to pass. Compare this with how many times this has actually come to pass.

Along with this, list the possible solutions and actions you could take to prevent the worst-case scenario.

Should this worst-case scenario actually happen, what steps can you take to cope with the fallout. What will you do to get through this difficult situation?

2. Be positive. List the *best-case scenarios*. Again, rate them on a scale of one through ten, the likeliness of this actually coming to pass.

If you are too focused on the negative, you will miss seeing the positive outcomes.

3. Now that you have listed both extremes, work on a neutral outcome. The one that is most likely to happen.

4. Worrying is helpful in that it forces you to prepare. However, worrying too much is counterproductive. Be aware of what you do and

do not have control over.

Pleasant Activity Scheduling

Do not forget to have fun. Actually, schedule this!

Make time for yourself.

The following exercise is geared at getting you to make time to enjoy the process of cognitive behavioral therapy.

Start by listing the days of the week. Choose an activity that you enjoy doing but either do not have time for or have neglected over the course of your life. It could be anything from reading a few pages from a novel, drawing a picture, taking photographs.

It can also be something that only takes ten

minutes out of your day. The point is to fully enjoy the time set aside. Even if it is something as simple as having your lunch outside, away from work responsibilities.

By doing this for yourself, you introduce more positivity into your life, and you create an overall better mood and experience from day to day. Your thinking will become less negative and you will see improvement.

Here are some examples of pleasant events. These are just for reference and you may use them as a starting point. If there are activities that you enjoy that do not appear, consider first if they are harmful or if they are helpful. If they are harmful but pleasant (for you) seek to avoid them or replace them with a similar event that will benefit you.

1. Meditate

2. Make plans with friends or family

3. Cooking

4. Taking care of plants

5. Drawing

6. Watching a movie

7. Wearing nice clothes

8. Go for a Walk

9. Exercise

10. Visit a Beauty parlor

11. Reading

Progressive Muscle Relaxation

This technique is often combined with meditation or as practice for those who also practice mindfulness. Used to help force the mind to empty by moving your focus elsewhere.

On the floor or a similarly stable and flat surface, lie on your back with your legs and arms slightly apart (think of a starfish).

Breathe deeply.

One by one, while still remaining in your starfish position, starting at your toes, tense the muscles as you move up our body. You can do this by flexing or pointing the toes.

Slowly move up the legs. Tense your calves while keeping your toe muscles tensed.

Then your thighs.

Your buttocks.

Take a moment to feel the muscles. Do you notice how they are interlinked with one another? Slowly release the muscles in reverse order. First the buttocks, thighs, calves, and finally the toes. Take a breath in and release. Let the tension release, melt away into the floor and away from you. Appreciate the stillness of your body.

Pull in on your abdominal muscles, imagining that you are pulling your belly button towards your back, to the floor beneath you.

Do remember to breathe steadily throughout this exercise, even when you have the urge to hold your breath.

Flex your fingers, push into the floor with the palms of your hands to activate the muscles in your forearms and upper arms.

Shrug your shoulders towards your ears and hold the position.

Scrunch up your face.

Hold this for a few moments and slowly release, again in reverse order. Relax the muscles in your face, shoulders, arms, hands, and abdomen. Take a breath in and release. Let the tension release, melt away into the floor and away from you. Appreciate the stillness of your body.

After practicing this a few times and you want to try a slightly more difficult exercise, do not release your muscles until you have tensed up every muscle group in your body.

Follow this up with relaxed breathing.

Relaxed Breathing

We often breathe shallowly which may lead not only to spikes in anxieties but also a host of health issues such as high blood pressure, shortness of breath, dizziness, headaches, and restlessness.

By breathing better, we increase the oxygen content carried by our blood which will not only improve your health but also improve your mood and concentration.

Set a time aside each morning for practice. A few short minutes is all you need, and you could do it first thing in the morning after you wake up and just before bed in the evening. Instead of reaching for your phone and social media, spend a few minutes regulating your breathing. Your mind will be less cluttered, and your sleep patterns should start improving.

While sitting or lying down comfortably, you will regulate your breathing.

Breathe in through your nose while slowly counting to eight.

Hold your breath for four counts.

Release the breath through the mouth for twelve counts.

Breathing exercises for stress

This exercise becomes more beneficial to you the more you use it and add it to your daily routine.

Find a spot to get comfortable. It can be standing up, sitting or lying down. Be sure to pick a position that will not restrict your breathing or distract you by being uncomfortable or even *too* comfortable which may cause you to drift off.

The aim is to de-stress consciously. To breathe out the negative emotions and the tension.

Loosen restrictive clothing.

Place your hands by your sides, palms up, with some space between your body and your hands. Bend your knees so your feet are flat on the floor, also slightly apart.

If you are sitting, place your arms on the chair arms and position your feet hip-width apart. Similarly, if you are standing.

Inhale through the nose. Let your breath reach deep down, expanding your chest to let in as much air as possible, but without forcing it.

Exhale through your mouth.

Inhale to the count of five, slow and steady. Again, if you cannot reach five counts, do not force it, go as high as you can go.

Do not hold your breath but instead release it again, slowly counting to five.

While going through this exercise, focus on your breath. Listen to it move through your lungs. Breathe uninterruptedly, continuously and slowly.

Repeat for three to five minutes each day.

Meditation

During meditation, you will begin to understand exactly how much activity lies in the brain; how busy it is in your head, even when you may feel like you are not doing anything to begin with. Adding meditation to your everyday practice you will learn how to recognize thoughts and how to change them.

The key here is to just let the thoughts happen. You observe them, separated from you, unaffecting you.

Do not worry too much about "how"; just sit, breathe, and the rest will soon follow. Do not focus on being perfect.

1. To start, take some time out of your day. Two minutes will do. You can always add extra time as you progress. It seems easy, right? You will learn how difficult it can be to stay still for even just two minutes, especially if you are used to being active.

2. It is easy to say, "I'll get to it" and "later". Set a time just after waking up in the morning before life gets busy. A few minutes of meditation instead of social media will bring great change.

3. Listen to how you are feeling, how your body is feeling. Are you exhausted? Anxious? Tired? Restless? This is meant as a check-up, not a test. There is no wrong answer here.

4. Count. Inhale, "one". Exhale, "two". Inhale, "three". Just focus on your breathing and counting as air flows in and out.

5. When your mind wanders, and it will, just slowly return your attention back to breathing. This is part of the process. You are busy training your mind to sit still. It is normal and with continuous practice, you will be able to keep your mind focused for longer. Start over at "one" again.

6. Be kind. Thoughts will distract you. Some of those thoughts will not be pleasant. Do

not judge yourself for them and do not condemn them for cropping up. Let them pass and return to counting your breaths.

7. Do not worry about doing things "wrong". There is no perfect way.

After you have spent some time practicing your meditation and extending the time spent on practice, instead of trying to clear your head or immediately returning to counting your breath, try focusing on the thoughts that arise. Observe them, feel them and let them go. Do the same with the next one.

Much like observing birds in your garden as they stop by briefly, peck at the dirt and flit about a bit before flying off. Stay with the thought that arises. In this way you will also learn how your own mind works; what causes it to get frustrated, what are you avoiding.

Life will undeniably get in the way; issues and emergencies will arise. Work around them. You can practice anywhere. Keep going, you've got this.

Should you feel you need some extra guided meditation, go for it. Whether it is at a community center with others or the use of audiobooks, find what works for you. Have a friend join you if you feel the need to. Even if it is just to check in with you after your practice to help keep you motivated and on track.

Remember to smile.

Yoga

Yoga for Anxiety

1. Reclined Bound Angle Pose

A restorative pose, this posture helps release the lower back.

It lowers blood pressure and provides relief from insomnia and anxiety.

It opens the hips and chest, increases blood circulation in the abdominal region, and calms the mind.

2. Legs Up the Wall

This pose is simple. Lie against the wall with your legs at a ninety-degree angle.

Place a folded blanket of other aid beneath your hips to elevate.

This pose drains the lymph nodes.

Ailments such as headaches, menstrual cramps, and lower back pain are targeted and relieved in this position.

Additionally, it relieves aching joints in the legs, as well as relieves swollen ankles and aids in digestion.

3. Child's Pose

Child's Pose is perfect after a long day.

This position is one of resting.

The position can be held for minutes at a time.

Focus on breathing.

It gently stretches your hips, ankles, thighs, and

shoulders.

It can assist in the reduction of stress and fatigue.

4. Forward Bend

This pose stimulates the liver and kidneys, and improves digestion; as well as relieve headaches, insomnia, stress, anxiety, and calms the brain.

It stretches the hips, hamstrings, and calves.

Excellent for someone who has a desk job and sits continuously.

5. Corpse Pose

Generally practiced at the end of a session, the Corpse Pose is known for the ability to calm the mind and relax the body. On the floor with your arms and legs slightly apart, allow yourself to relax and melt into the floor.

The goal is stillness of the body. Feel your breath.

Relax and unwind.

Other benefits include lowering blood pressure and reducing the prevalence of fatigue.

Yoga for Stress

Child's Pose

1. Start on all fours with your legs and knees together.

2. Sit back on your heels and fold yourself forward, resting your belly on your thighs completely.

3. Stretch our arms above your head, touching your forehead to the mat.

4. Breathe through the stretch, attempting to lengthen your shoulders and torso.

Downward Dog

1. From a kneeling position, walk your hands out in front of you, straightening your legs.

2. Push your hips back into Downward Dog, creating a V-shape with your body.

Wide-Legged Fold

1. From Downward Dog, bring your right leg up to the front of your mat in between your hands in a lunge.

2. Straighten the right leg.

3. Slowly pivot your body to the left, your toes should now be facing the same direction

4. Release your head down and rest your hands in between your legs on the mat.

5. Hold this pose for a few counts. Breathe.

Headstand

1. From the wide-legged fold, transition back into a lunge.

2. Bring your legs back into a high plank position.

3. Lower your knees down to the ground so that you are on your hands and knees.

4. Drop your forearms to the mat and lock your fingers together.

5. Lean your head into your hands.

6. Start to shift your weight onto your arms and head.

7. Lift your legs towards the ceiling, keeping your core tight and your legs as straight as possible.

8. Hold the pose for a long as possible but aim to increase this duration over time.

9. Slowly bring your legs back down to the ground.

10. Slide back into child's pose, extending the arms ahead of you.

Pigeon Pose Right Leg

1. From child's pose, return your position to your hands and knees.

2. Bring your right knee up to rest behind your right hand.

3. Slide your foot out from under your right

leg.

4. Push your left leg out behind you.

5. Slowly fold yourself forward over your knee.

Pigeon Pose Left Leg

1. Lift up out of Pigeon pose and return to your hands and knees.

2. Bring your left knee up to rest behind your left hand.

3. Slide your foot out from under your left leg.

4. Push your right leg out behind you.

5. Slowly fold yourself forward over your knee.

Supported Bridge

1. Rise up into a seated position. You should have a block or ball ready for this movement.

2. Have the ball or block behind you as you stretch your legs out in front of you, still remaining seated.

3. Support your upper body with your arm by your side.

4. Lift and lean back over the ball or block.

5. Rest on the block.

6. Extend your arms at the sides to a T-position, keeping your feet flexed.

7. Should the ball or block be small enough that your buttocks are still touching the

floor, slowly raise your legs into the air, keeping them together.

8. Hold.

Yoga for Depression

Savasana (Corpse Pose)

Savasana, also called the corpse pose, is a simple pose that works on the mind as well as the body.

This pose explores self-awareness and mindfulness.

The pose is performed at the end of each yoga session to bring about a calmer, and relaxed state of being.

How to Do the Corpse Pose:

Lie flat on your back on the yoga mat.

Close your eyes.

Rest both arms comfortably by your sides, palms up.

Knees kept slightly apart, point your toes outwards.

Consciously relax every part of your body, starting from the toes.

Gradually moving upwards, relax each body part in turn.

Keep your breathing slow and relaxed while doing so.

Remain in the pose for 10-20 minutes.

Release the pose in *Sukhasana* or Easy Pose.

Sukhasana (Easy Pose)

Sukhasana is a highly effective seated pose. Generally used during intense meditation, it is an easy pose that will relax the mind and body and corrects the body's alignment.

The pose should ideally be performed on an empty stomach in the morning.

How to do the Easy Pose:

Sit on your mat in a comfortable position with your legs stretched out ahead of you.

Slowly and gently bend each leg at the knee.

Keep the feet below the leg.

Align the torso with the hips.

Keep your spine straight and your core tight.

Distribute the body weight evenly on each hip.

Rest your arms and hands on your knees.

Close your eyes and breathe deeply.

The pose has no time limitation, but you could start small by limiting this time to three minutes a day.

Ūrdhva Mukha Svānāsana (Upward Facing Dog Pose)

Upward facing dog opens the heart and dispels pent-up negative emotions held in the chest. These include anxiety and depression. The pose helps regulate breathing and restores clarity to the mind. Regular practice will have you feeling more open, eager, and relaxed; embracing life and be better at facing upcoming challenges.

How to Do the Upward Facing Dog Pose:

Lie flat on your stomach on the mat.

Keep the balls of the feet facing upwards and the toes pointed.

Bring both palms to your shoulders.

Gently lift your upper body, keeping your hips on the floor.

Lengthen the entire body from head to toe.

Take deep breaths while holding the pose in the air, face drawn upwards to embrace positivity and hope.

Mindfulness

Mindfulness: TAKING CONTROL OF YOUR ATTENTION AND THOUGHTS.

The active decision to remain in a moment and not to be distracted by thoughts or emotions that could control you instead of the other way around.

In order to be in a mindful state, we have to be able to separate our internal processes that are tied to thought and emotion.

There are two main states of mind you can find yourself in, two states you can define and categorize your thoughts through. This will help you differentiate between a *reasoned* thought or emotion and an *emotional* thought or reaction.

The Reason Mind

This is the way you think or believe you ought to act based on a certain emotion and situation.

Often how society dictated one should respond.

The Emotion Mind

Exactly as described. Your emotions do not have brains, they just are. You feel so intensely that you act out of instinct.

A Wise Mind as explained by Linehan (1993) requires you to understand both types and bring the two together. A wise mind is one where you are aware that while you are angry right now, the best course of action is to calmly express how you feel and extract yourself from the situation.

There needs to be a willingness to act with a "wise mind". You need to cultivate a willing response to each situation. Willingness is doing exactly what is needed in each situation, in a modest way by focusing on effectiveness.

Willingness is listening to your "wise mind". This needs you to carefully become aware of how your emotions and thoughts intertwine and affect you.

Willingness is allowing awareness of everything around you, physical and emotional. Contradicting this is being "willful". This implies that you are acting out of spite and negative emotion. Willfulness is refusing to acknowledge and tolerate the situation. It is in you trying to FIX the situation rather than attempting to understand it.

What skills: What to do when an emotion arises.

OBSERVE: Do not judge the emotion but be curious about it. Take note of how long the emotion lasts, does it change?

DESCRIBE: Use your words. Describe the emotion in a matter-of-fact way. It is just a thought or a feeling, there is no need to embellish the emotion or the situation to have it appear worse or more impactful than it is. Avoid describing with emotional words. "I hate her for failing me." Try to let go of who is right and who is wrong. Adapt the way you describe the emotion and the difference is felt.

Participate: The idea is to get lost in an activity and to lose time. Do not watch the clock or be worried about other things that need to be done immediately. Being mindful means to be in the moment. Practice your skills until they are a part of you.

How skills: How to go about reacting to your emotions in a mindful way.

Take a NON-JUDGEMENTAL STANCE on the situation. Just observe, there is no need to evaluate or judge the emotion. Accept each moment as it comes - fully. It is neither wrong nor right to feel a certain way, emotions just are. Let go of anger and vengeance.

Strive to be MINDFULLY IN THE MOMENT by doing one thing at a time. If you are doing the dishes, **do** the dishes. Focus on the task at hand. Watch how the sponge or cloth moves over the object; watch how the soap bubbles form and get washed away when you rinse.

Give each task your full and undivided attention, do not worry about what is for supper, or what still needs to be done for the rest of the day - there will be time enough for that. Let go of distractions and focus your mind.

Keep focusing on what works for you. Meet the expectation of the situation you are in and not the one you are hoping it could be or the one you want.

Mindfulness is the ability to be present and aware in each situation; aware of where you are and what you are doing.

It is the act of simply observing.

While the mindfulness skill is something we inherently possess; its benefits and ease of access become more apparent the more you practice.

Any time that you change your level of awareness, whether it is by acknowledging what you are experiencing physically, for example, focusing on what you see, hear, or smell; or if it is taking stock of your own thoughts and feelings within that moment, those actions are considered being mindful.

The goal of mindfulness is to become aware of exactly how our brains work: our mental and emotional processes that govern our actions.

Benefits of Mindfulness

1. Mindfulness reduces overthinking.

One of the most common symptoms that goes hand in hand with anxiety, fear, and stress is overthinking. When you start to worry about something, your brain has been programmed to keep with it and attempt to solve it but being unable to let go until the task is complete. Sometimes this causes a loop within the brain where the situation or thought keeps playing over and over in an attempt to resolve it.

By practicing mindfulness or adding it to your daily routine, you will have fewer situations as described above. Not only is it possible to reduce the impact that anxiety has on you, but it could also improve other mental aspects like memory improvement. (Chambers et al)

2. Mindfulness alleviates stress.

Due to the increasingly complicated and complex nature of society, the pressure to perform is increasing and we are subject to suffering a lot of stress. This contributes to a wide variety of health problems. Mindfulness can reduce stress and the negative health symptoms associated with it.

3. Mindfulness helps with emotional responsiveness.

A common reason for people to incorporate mindfulness into their daily routine is to become less emotionally reactive. Being able to stand firm mentally and emotionally when life throws adversity your way (Ortner, Et al).

Mindfulness meditation has allowed participants to distance themselves and their emotions from an upsetting situation and remain focused on a different, mentally engaging task.

4. Mindfulness reduces anxiety.

Practicing mindfulness on a regular basis, assists in rewiring your brain in order to refocus your attention. Being able to identify negative thoughts for what they are, it will equip you with the tools to negate anxiety associated with recurring worrying.

5. Mindfulness improves sleep.

The relaxation response resulting from practicing mindfulness assists in easing stress-related health issues such as sleeplessness and insomnia, pain, depression, and high blood pressure.

6. Mindfulness slows down the progression of brain degeneration.

The effect and occurrence of age-related cognitive disorders, such as dementia and Alzheimer's can be reduced or slowed down by the regular practice of mindfulness meditation.

7. Mindfulness enhances creativity.

Mindfulness as part of a daily routine creates a balance between the different hemispheres within the brain. The creative and analytical are put into harmony it one another. This balance is required in order to be more creative.

8. Mindfulness reduces feelings of loneliness.

Feelings of loneliness can be linked to an increased risk of anxiety, depression, and even a shortened lifespan due to physical degeneration and illness. Mindfulness reduces these feelings of loneliness and reduces the risks associated with it.

9. Mindfulness increases body satisfaction and positivity.

Mindfulness meditation requires self-love without the appearance of judgment, and complete acceptance of yourself as you are.

When you are unsatisfied with your body or your looks, you are preoccupied with these thoughts instead of focusing on being non-judgmental.

By practicing mindfulness, you begin to experience moments free of judgment, and with regular practice, personal judgments are also reduced.

10. Mindfulness assists with illness recovery.

Mindfulness reduces the physical symptoms associated with stress and decreases the effects of negative experiences and thoughts overall. By reducing the occurrence of anxiety and stress, the body's self-healing response gets a chance to work.

11. Mindfulness helps lower risk of burnout.

Burnout manifests as depression, aggression, decreased cognitive performance, and decreased motivation. It is physical and emotional exhaustion. It occurs when the body and mind have been constantly active, stressing, problem-solving, etc. without rest or a proper chance of relaxation. This condition has been associated with a significant increase in physical and mental health issues such as increased blood pressure, heart disease, anxiety, and depression.

Mindfulness Meditation "How To"

1. Set yourself a time and a prompt for your practice. It does not necessarily have to be at the same time each day. The prompt acts as a trigger or starting point for your practice. It can while drinking your tea, walking the dog or even brushing your teeth. It will send your brain a signal that it is time to quiet down.

2. Find a quiet place to go.

A quiet, relaxed space in your house, outside or even in the car. You may even have a space already set up for this specifically. Location matters less than environment as long as it is quiet, and you will not be interrupted.

3. Get comfortable.

Notice your body. Be sure it is in a position that

you are comfortable in and able to remain in. Being uncomfortable will cause you to be distracted.

Allow your spine to relax into its natural state. Comfort is of utmost importance.

4. Soften your gaze.

You do not need to close your eyes but do allow your eyelids to droop. "Unfocusing" your gaze allows you to see without being distracted by what you are seeing.

5. Relax your entire body.

Mentally scan over your muscles. Release any tension you may be holding.

6. Focus on your breath.

Think about your breathing and the air flowing in

and out. Feel your breath. Think about the physical sensations that occur as you inhale and exhale; the rising and falling of your chest. Follow the sensation of your breathing. Follow it in and follow it out.

7. Notice when your mind has wandered.

It will wander. Do not be negative about this. Simply return to focusing on your breathing. Be kind to yourself. Do not judge too harshly or obsess over the thoughts you find yourself lost in. Just come back.

8. When you are done.

Set a time limit. If you are just starting out, a shorter time limit will be more beneficial than a long one.

There exists no right or wrong length of time

needed to complete this practice. It could be as short as two minutes or as long as an hour. The benefits depend on you.

After your practice, slowly return to consciousness and your present moment and surroundings and lift your gaze.

Take your time to return to moment. Acknowledge how your body feels in that moment as you move each part.

Observing-Your-Breath Exercises

Focus your attention on your breath coming in and out. Use these exercises as a way to center yourself in the moment and take control of your mind.

1. Deep breathing: Lie on your back. Breathe

deep and evenly; focus on the movement of your stomach and chest. As you breathe in allow your stomach to rise as you take in the breath - fill your lungs completely. Exhale longer than you inhale - empty your lungs without forcing it too much. Repeat for ten breaths.

2. Measure your breath by your footsteps. Go on a walk and measure each breath with each step while breathing normally. Begin to extend your breath by an extra step. For example, if you inhale on each left and right, extend the duration by making it two lefts and a right. Let the breathing continue naturally, do not force the breath longer than you are able to maintain without tiring yourself out. Continue for ten breaths.

3. Counting your breath. While sitting comfortably, as you inhale be aware that "I am inhaling, ONE." When you exhale, be aware, "I am exhaling, TWO." (Linehan, 1993) Breathe from the stomach and continue being mindful of your counting ad breathing and after you have reached the count of ten, return to ONE. Should you lose count, return to ONE.

4. While listening to music, you can breathe along to the music, light and easy. Be aware of the music; the rhythm, the movement, and the motions the music is evoking. Do not get lost in the music but appreciate it and let it anchor you in mindfulness.

5.

Emotional Regulation

MYTHS

Myths are stories we believe solely because they are part of our lives. Myths are unique. Myths are nurtured and developed by our friends and families. They are a part of our culture.

They are sometimes hard to identify or change, especially if they are deeply ingrained, like showing respect to your elders even in a situation where this person does not reciprocate or act in a way that does not dignify the respect. These myths shape our thoughts and often are the cause of our anxieties:

"I must do everything right or I am not competent"

"I am not a good person, therefore I do not

deserve good things"

Thought Regulation

Observing and describing your thoughts. Use these exercises to help identify your thoughts and their causes. These are often tied to emotions, however, use the exercises separately. Use your journal to keep track of these exercises.

1. What is the event that has caused the thought? (This may be a bumper bashing or a stranger being rude to you in a shopping center)

2. What are your feelings about the *thought?* What is the intensity of these emotions? (Are you mad/sad/glad/scared/ashamed)

3. What are your feelings and emotions about the *situation?* (Are you mad/sad/glad/scared/ashamed)

4. Make a list of your thoughts in the situation. Make a list of thoughts you had before the situation. List what your thoughts were after.

5. What did you notice as a MUST about the situation? (A must is something you must have done in order to better the situation, the ideal response, or what would have been expected in a normal setting)

6. What did you notice that you should have done or said? (Instead of yelling out of anger, I should have tried to keep calm)

7. What do you think other people should have done in the same situation? (They should have not

provoked me)

8. Choose one should on your list (can be both based on the situation, a personal should, or relating to others). Now take that one should and change it into a non-judgment. This is to teach you how to extract from the situation and view it without emotion. For example, if you choose to evaluate how they should have acted, you can change it in a way that removes you from the situation.

It prompts the question of whether the other person was acting the way they did because of you or because it was what was expected, given the situation.

Whenever you are evaluating your emotions or thoughts, consider that you have access to and should often make use of strength-building statements. Be sure to add these in during your practice in order to assist in helping cope when you start to doubt yourself.

1. What is the worst that can happen? (We do often ask ourselves the very same question, sometimes jokingly. However, in this case, ask it truthfully and without bias, without emotion.)

2. Feelings may be painful but not permanent!

3. It gets easier each time I practice. (It may be hard and feel like you are not making much progress but keep going!)

4. I am not going to let a lapse get in my way. I am going to make progress towards my goal.

5. Feeling that I cannot do something is not the same as actually NOT doing it. (Even if you feel

like you are unmotivated; if you choose to do it anyway, you are still making progress.)

6. Good job! I am staying in the situation even though it's hard.

7. I am going to make it.

8. I can ask for help.

9. Knowing *when* to ask is a skill.

10. I am unique, and I have unique reactions. Only I can determine how I should feel.

11. Feelings are not right or wrong - they just are.

12. Feelings of certainty are not same as truth.

13. Painful emotions happens for a reason - they are my sources of information and help direct my thoughts and actions in better directions.

14. Urges are a natural part of emotion and a natural part of being human. When I have an urge, it does not mean I have to act on the emotions.

Observing and describing emotions is a way to get familiar with them. In your journal, write down each of these prompts and answer them as thoroughly as possible and in as much detail as possible.

1. What is the name of your main emotion? Attempt to identify the primary emotion.

2. What was the event or situation in which the emotion occurred?

3. What are your assumptions/beliefs/myths about the situation? What did you assume about the other person? What did you believe before

and during the event? What myth is part of this interaction? (Remember to refer back to what myths are and be sure to be as honest as possible).

4. What sensations do you notice in your body? (Take careful note of how your body reacts to the situation and relative emotions. Heart rate, perspiration, stomach pains, etc.)

5. What is your body language with the emotion (posture, facial expression).

6. What action urges do you have? (What do you want to do - this is the behavior that is triggered by the emotional situation)

7. What will be the outcome of you acting on this urge? Will acting in this way bring you closer or further away from your goal?

Consider that there may be another behavior that would work better in that situation than the urge you have - what is it?

8. What will be the outcome of skillful behavior in this instance? List the pros and cons. Why would it be bad and why would it be good? Even applying skillful behaviors may not have the desired outcome or they may not make you feel good immediately due to the high amount of stress tied to the action.

Taking steps to reduce your vulnerability:

1. STAYING STRONG - healthy habits are part of managing mood swings, depression, and anger. Select one skill you want to work on in a week and

monitor your goal. Should you wish to be more flexible, make it a new skill each day but be sure to monitor your progress towards your goal. If it becomes too much, you have the option of changing your schedule. It is adaptable to your needs and will yield better results in the end.

2. SLEEP - as much as you *need* to. However, be careful that you do not oversleep or restrict your sleep needs. Just as much as your body needs; a general rule of thumb is eight hours a night.

3. Take any medication that is prescribed. Whether it is flu medication or medication given post-surgery, be sure to take them to improve healing and recovery.

4. Resist recreational drugs such as alcohol and marijuana, as well as other street drugs.

5. Once a day do something that gives you the feeling of accomplishment and of control. If you get that feeling from washing dishes and cleaning the kitchen without disruption, then you do that. If it is gardening in the early morning, do it. Be sure to set a time aside so that it is not interrupted by something "more urgent".

6. Live a healthy, balanced lifestyle. Eating healthier will not only increase general well-being but will also reduce intestinal inflammation, mood swings, and weight gain. Do not, however, make a decision based around emotion. Do not under eat because "I am not hungry right now" or over eat because "I need to eat something because I am stressed out."

7. Plan a structured activity once a day for at least twenty minutes. This can be walking the dog,

swimming, jogging, or attending the gym.

Improving on your sleep

Sleep is an integral part of life and well-being. Below are some helpful tips in how you will be able to improve on the quality and the quantity of sleep you are getting.

1. Sleep only as much as you need to feel refreshed. A rule of thumb is to get eight hours of sleep a night, however, this number changes based on personal requirement, certain medications, and general activity. By restricting time in bed, i.e. not staying in bed all day, you can deepen your sleep. Adversely, by spending too much time in bed, your sleep will be shallow and will leave you feeling tired all day, no matter how much sleep you got.

2. Get up at the same time each day. By creating a habit, you will reprogram your body and reset your biological clock, making the need for excessive sleep null and void in the long run. The human body is remarkably resilient, just hang in there.

3. Exercise regularly but at least three hours before bed. The energy release and spike will affect your sleep pattern and keep you up later than scheduled.

4. Ensure that your bedroom is at a comfortable temperature, as well as dark and noise free. The light stimulation negatively affects sleep. Noises could wake you and disturb your sleep. Some people are lighter sleepers, so this is more important to them.

5. Eat regular meals and do not go to bed hungry.

6. Avoid consuming excess liquids before bed.

7. Cut down on caffeine and like products.

8. Avoid alcohol.

9. Smoking may disturb sleep as nicotine is stimulant. Try not to wake up in the night to go smoke and avoid smoking before bed.

10. Do not take your problems with you to bed. Schedule a time in the day in order to plan your next day and routine and to evaluate your progress.

11. Try to use the bedroom only for sleeping. Do not go there to work or to hide.

12. Do not TRY to fall asleep. Accept sleep as it comes. Forcing sleep causes disappointment and irritation which will delay the onset of sleep.

13. Put your clock under the bed or turn it around so that you cannot see and keep track of the time. Clock watching leads to frustration, worry, and exhaustion.

14. Avoid naps. Simple. If you cannot, at least try to keep your naps restricted to a 25-minute power nap and be sure to take your nap between 1:00 PM and 3:00 PM.

Conclusion

After having completed this program, as well as the accompanying exercises, you should feel comfortable in tackling the difficult situations in your life with confidence. The tools set out here are aimed at helping you approach your fears and anxieties and adapt your negative thinking to improve your ability to deal with your own stressors.

The difficulties addressed in this book are a small number of issues that can be addressed using cognitive behavioral therapy, however, should you feel that your problem is too large for you to handle on your own, remember that you are not alone.

Support centers are available to you and a quick

search on the internet will be able to direct you to

the people who can help.

Author's Note

If there was one thing that you learned from reading this book, what would it be? All you need is that one key learning to take you to the next steps in your journey to becoming more self-aware of your personal strengths and weaknesses.

The only way to keep this learning alive is by sharing it with a friend or a colleague who can benefit from it. In doing so, you are creating a network of people who can keep the conversation alive around the topic that you've just read.

In the end of all this, I hope that you have found your golden nugget/s throughout reading this book. Your success is my success.

Cheers,

www.ingramcontent.com/pod-product-compliance
Lightning Source LLC
Chambersburg PA
CBHW031057250726
48655CB00004B/1475